IMAGES
of America

WORLD WAR I
ON THE
VIRGINIA PENINSULA

T. Parker Host Sr. was a successful Newport News ship agent when the United States declared war against Germany. He joined the U.S. Army as an aviator but arrived in France after the Armistice ended the war. Host was later elected to the Newport News City Council and served as the city's mayor from 1940 to 1942. When World War II erupted, Host resigned his position as mayor and rejoined the U.S. Army Air Corps.

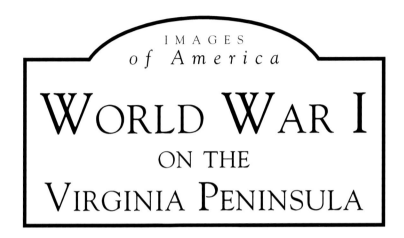

IMAGES
of America

WORLD WAR I
ON THE
VIRGINIA PENINSULA

John V. Quarstein

With Sarah Goldberger, J. Michael Moore, and Tim Smith, Photo Editors

ARCADIA
PUBLISHING

Published by Arcadia Publishing
Charleston, South Carolina

Printed in the United States of America

Library of Congress Catalog Card Number: 98-88695

For all general information contact Arcadia Publishing at:
Telephone 843-853-2070
Fax 843-853-0044
E-Mail sales@arcadiapublishing.com
For customer service and orders:
Toll-Free 1-888-313-2665

Visit us on the Internet at www.arcadiapublishing.com

On the cover: Pictured are the men and machines of Motor Truck Company (MTC) 409 at Camp Hill in Newport News, Virginia, on September 29, 1918. The unit was commanded by First Lieutenant A.B. Camper. Panoramic photographs, like this one of the 409th MTC, were produced by the hundreds by photographers at Cheyne Studios of Hampton, G.L. Hall Optical of Norfolk, and Holladay Studios of Newport News. Griffith Studio photographed ships as they arrived in port to sell to the soldiers as they disembarked from "The Ship that Brought Me Home."

In this 1910 view, battleships of the U.S. North Atlantic Fleet steam past Fort Monroe.

CONTENTS

Captain M.A. McKinney commanded all aerial photography and training for Langley Field's U.S. Army School of Aerial Photographic Reconnaissance. McKinney was a pre-war commercial photographer who established and commanded Langley's Photography School during and after World War I. Aerial photographic reconnaissance was an important duty assigned to the infant U.S. Air Service. Intelligence gathering via aerial photography was virtually unknown in the United States prior to its entry into the conflict. Training schools, such as Langley Field's School of Aerial Photographic Reconnaissance, were therefore established to bring the American photographic intelligence-gathering activities on par with those of the Allies. Observers had to be schooled in terrain recognition, camera techniques, and machine gun operation. Weapon training was of great importance since all flights were completed over enemy territory. Photographic surveys provided long-distance oblique views of enemy positions and proved to be of great value in the preparation of detailed plans for attacks against German defensive lines.

INTRODUCTION

When the "Guns of August" erupted across Europe in 1914, the Virginia Peninsula was the home of two small, but growing, communities: Hampton and Newport News. These towns had finally emerged from the ashes of the Civil War during the last two decades of the 19th century. The seafood industry blossomed in the 1890s, thanks to the ingenuity and enterprise of men like James McMenamin and J.S. Darling. Hampton became a leading center for oysters and crabs. Northern entrepreneur and railroad adventurer Collis P. Huntington also recognized the Peninsula's promise of economic vitality. Huntington's Chesapeake & Ohio Railroad, completed in 1881, connected Hampton Roads with the heartland of America. The city of Newport News was built almost overnight. In 1886, the flourishing port prompted Huntington to create the Newport News Shipbuilding and Dry Dock Company. The shipyard, reinforced with U.S. Navy contracts, became the Peninsula's major industry.

World War I, however, was a European war 3,000 miles away from Hampton Roads, and few Peninsula residents thought they would be drawn into the conflict. The Europeans expected a short war, but the machine gun and other new forms of technology turned the conflict into a war of attrition. Trench warfare marred the landscape as countless soldiers died in the muddy trenches.

The war seemed far away, despite the internment of German freighters and commerce raiders in Hampton Roads. These ships piqued local interest, but it was the sinking of the *Lusitania* on May 7, 1915, that made the war a reality to Peninsula residents. Among the 124 Americans who died when the luxury liner was torpedoed was Albert Hopkins, president of the shipyard. He was the first of many from the Peninsula who lost their lives during this bloody conflict.

Anti-German sentiment began mounting after the *Lusitania*'s sinking, and the Peninsula prepared for war. Local soldiers in Battery D, 111th Field Artillery, participated in the Mexican Punitive Expedition commanded by Brigadier General John J. Pershing. The Army Appropriation Act of 1916 resulted in the purchase of land along the Back River that would eventually become Langley Field.

Even before the air field was officially opened, the United States declared war against Germany on April 6, 1917, over the expansion of unrestricted submarine warfare. Fort Monroe quickly became headquarters for harbor defense and the Coast Artillery Training Center. This prompted the construction of a new training area for heavy artillery at Camp Eustis on Mulberry Island in Warwick County. Fort Wool was revitalized and garrisoned. Mine defenses were created, and a submarine net was laid to protect the entrance to Hampton Roads from German submarine attack.

Shortly after the declaration of war, the Army assumed operation of the port from the C&O Railroad and began acquiring properties in Newport News and Warwick County for troop staging areas. The Hampton Roads Port of Embarkation consisted of four staging camps. Camps Hill, Stuart, Alexander, and Morrison would send 261,820 men overseas and welcome home 441,146 veterans.

Beyond Langley Field, the Peninsula became the site for other aviation facilities. In 1915, the Curtiss Flying School was established at the Small Boat Harbor in Newport News. The school soon became the Atlantic Coast Aeronautical Station and trained noted aviators such as Colonel Billy Mitchell and ace H.M. "Buck" Gallop. The Army Air Service Balloon Observation School was established at Fort Eustis.

Shipbuilding boomed on the Peninsula during the war. By 1919, the Newport News Shipbuilding and Dry Dock Company's payroll increased to 12,500. These workers repaired over 1,000 merchant vessels and constructed the battleship *Missouri* and 25 destroyers. The most elaborate and patriotic event during the war was Liberty Launching Day on July 4, 1918. Three destroyers—the *Haraden*, the *Abbot*, and the *Thomas*—were launched.

Other local shipyards contributed to the war effort. The Newcomb Lifeboat Company on Sunset Creek in Hampton received a contract to build 10 wooden subchasers. Two vessels, the *Kahoka* and the *Luray*, were launched before the war ended.

The bustle of troops marching along the avenues and the hammers ringing at area shipyards prompted Peninsula residents to cater to every soldier's need by participating in the patriotic events staged by community leaders. The War Camp Community Service established Red Circle Clubs at every military camp, and the YMCA built Hostess Houses to entertain the troops. The Red Cross organized a Canteen Corps to greet soldiers at dockside with refreshments, and the Red Cross Motor Corps served patients throughout the Peninsula. Other organizations, such as the Salvation Army, Jewish Welfare Board, and American Library Association, provided various services to the soldiers. The Girls' Patriotic League knitted socks, rolled bandages, and attended countless dances, while Boy Scouts went door to door selling war bonds.

The Peninsula was a boomtown during the war. Newport News nearly doubled in population, expanding from 26,246 residents in 1910 to 47,013 in 1920. All of the workers needed housing. The Emergency Fleet Corporation, an agency of the War Shipping Board, financed several major projects, including Hilton Village, the first government-subsidized, planned community.

When the war ended, the Peninsula immediately began welcoming home the nation's veterans. The Newport Victory Arch, hastily constructed of wood and plaster, was dedicated on April 13, 1919. A little over a month later, local boys serving in the 29th "Blue and Gray" Division marched through the Victory Arch during two joyous celebrations welcoming the soldiers home.

World War I was now truly over for the Peninsula. The community had become the "harbor of a thousand ships" and several community leaders envisioned that Hampton Roads would soon rival New York as America's greatest port. Yet, the war ended too quickly, and the United States refused to ratify the League of Nations. The nation turned its back on Europe and sought to disarm. The Peninsula's economy, already troubled by a post-war slump, was further devastated when the 1922 Washington Naval Treaty was signed. Consequently, the U.S. Government canceled over $70 million in Navy contracts at the shipyard, and many residents feared that the shipyard might close. Another decade would pass before world affairs, threatened by militaristic dictatorships, would restore the Peninsula's economic vitality.

One

MARCHING INTO A
NEW CENTURY

During the almost 50-year span between the end of the Civil War and World War I, the Virginia Peninsula underwent a remarkable transformation. Two cities, Hampton and Newport News, emerged after the Civil War. Northern entrepreneurs, like Collis P. Huntington, recognized that the waters surrounding the Peninsula offered tremendous economic opportunity. Huntington established a railroad on the Peninsula that fostered the rapid growth of Newport News as a port and shipbuilding center. Others, like J.S. Darling, used the accessibility provided by the railroad and port to turn Hampton into a major seafood center. As documented by this image of Washington Avenue, Newport News's main thoroughfare, the Peninsula's rapid transition from farmland to factory was amazing.

From the time the English colonists arrived in 1607, agriculture was the mainstay of the Virginia Peninsula's economy. Tobacco was king, and it flourished as a cash crop during the 17th and 18th centuries. This export brought tremendous wealth and influence to the lower Peninsula planters; unfortunately, it also ruined the soil's productivity. As a result, the region became a backwater community, losing its population to westward expansion until the introduction of scientific farming in the 19th century. "Those who have adopted the four-field system," Daniel Prentiss Curtis of Mulberry Island wrote in the 1850s, "look forward with great expectation of success, both in improvement and profit. Our crops of corn are very promising." One of the many prosperous farms on the Peninsula was the Smith Farm, located near the Warwick Court House. This photograph was taken in 1915.

George Benjamin West of Newport News Point considered the Peninsula to be a pastoral paradise and believed that "no one could desire to live in a more favored place . . ." One soldier passing through the region called the Peninsula "a veritable Garden of Eden with numerous fine homes and beautifully cultivated lands." West described this agrarian wonderland in an address he presented to the "Pioneers of Newport News" in 1914: "Corn, oats, wheat and sweet potatoes were the principal crops raised. The land was particularly adapted to sweets and this was the chief money crop, and every farmer cultivated from four to forty acres. They [were] sold by the bushel and shipped in schooners . . . In 1860 when the New York steamships from Richmond stopped to take trucks direct to New York . . . Irish potatoes, tomatoes, and other trucks were raised and the sweets were then shipped in barrels . . . Only the larger farmers raised wheat and oats . . . and they shipped in pungies to Baltimore and Richmond." The above scene depicts the July 4, 1911 celebration on the Bailey Farm in Warwick County. The fruits of the land apparently made for a wonderful lifestyle.

The agrarian society may have provided a good lifestyle for some on the Peninsula but it did not sustain the majority of the population. Limited educational facilities, poor transportation systems, and the lack of viable commercial centers offered few economic opportunities. Yorktown, once a flourishing port, had become a virtual backwater community. The tracks laid for the Yorktown Centennial Celebration, seen in this photograph, were quickly removed.

Dynamic railroad developer Collis P. Huntington forever changed the Peninsula's landscape. Walter A. Post, one of Huntington's agents and later Newport News's first mayor, described Newport News Point when he first arrived on November 26, 1880: "Two houses occupied by white families and a few huts furnishing homes for Negroes were scattered over the area now comprised within the limits of the city. Scattered around on all sides were earthworks and other evidences of the late conflict between the states and desolation was everywhere. We were immediately struck with the magnificent possibilities afforded by the harbor and while we were impressed by the judgment and foresight manifested by Mr. Huntington, we wondered why this point had not long before been recognized and utilized as a site for a city. Early in December we began the work of construction and soon the scene of desolation was transformed into one of activity."

Collis P. Huntington moved to California during the Gold Rush and made a fortune building railroads. After completing the Central Pacific, a portion of the first transcontinental railroad, Huntington returned to Virginia. He believed that there was "no better place for a city" than Newport News Point and selected the site to become the eastern terminus of the Chesapeake & Ohio Railroad. Huntington had recently acquired the bankrupt railroad and sought to use it as a development tool. Realizing that the Peninsula offered an opportunity to control all aspects of a new city's growth, he had agents of the Huntington holding company, aptly called the Old Dominion Land Company, begin acquiring land in the 1870s. The actual construction of the line connecting Newport News with Richmond started in 1880, as seen in this c. 1890 photo.

The last spike completing the C&O was driven on October 16, 1881, just in time to carry passengers to the Centennial Celebration at Yorktown. A new station, pictured here, was built and named in honor of the nearby Lee Hall Mansion. A special temporary track was laid to Yorktown, but was taken up immediately following the celebration, as Huntington did not want to help any potential competitors on the Peninsula. The first run from Newport News to Lee Hall was made on the morning of October 19, 1881. The train was pulled by a locomotive delivered to Newport News Point on a schooner. Regular service commenced on May 1, 1882.

Concurrent with the construction of the railroad, a new port city was built on the Peninsula. Two deep water piers were completed in 1882—a 700-foot-long cargo pier and an 825-foot-long coal pier. The water was 30-feet deep at the end of the pier, and six vessels were able to load simultaneously. The piers handled over 100,000 tons of cargo during the first year of operation. Exports and imports exceeded $3.7 million the next year. By 1897, more than 600 vessels cleared the port with cargo valued at over $23.5 million.

Huntington continued to expand the port's capabilities. A grain elevator with a capacity of 1.5 million bushels was completed in 1883, and a second was built in 1902. The two dominated the Newport News skyline as long as they stood. Grain Elevator A, built of wood and sheet metal, was destroyed in a devastating fire in 1915.

Seafood, a natural resource of the Tidewater region, was slow to develop on the Peninsula as a major industry. The arrival of the C&O Railroad and refrigeration cars during the decades following the Civil War transformed local oysters, clams, and crabs into an important commodity. Watermen rushed to get their perishable harvest to market as quickly as possible. The C&O established a spur line to Hampton and built a station called Oyster Point between the Deep Creek and Menchville harbors to facilitate the shipment of succulent Hampton Bar and James River oysters. Primitive refrigerated boxcars, with straw-covered dry ice placed at each end so cool air circulated over the perishable goods, maximized the distance at which fresh seafood could be delivered.

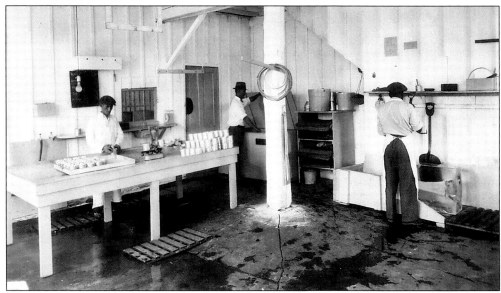

Two Hamptonians helped to change the seafood industry with their ingenuity. In 1878, James McMenamin perfected a preservation process for canning crabmeat. Within two years, McMenamin and Company was one of the largest firms in Hampton, with sales of $5 million and 350 people employed during the season. Samuel S. Coston, owner of the Coston Company, developed a method to ship fresh crab meat. Once picked, the crab meat was placed in metal cans with small holes in the bottom then packed in ice for shipment. Captain J.S. Darling operated an oyster packing firm that became the largest in the world. Darling rented 350 acres of oyster grounds on the Hampton Bar. He employed 160 shuckers, 100 men for the operation of two steam dredges, and he owned over 25 log canoes. The oyster shells outside the Darling plant often reached a height of over 50 feet. This 1915 photograph is an interior view of the Watkins Seafood Packing Plant in Hampton.

The seafood industry revitalized Hampton and several other small communities on the Peninsula. While oysters and crabs were the prime market catch, other fish like sturgeon and menhaden were harvested. Fish camps were erected along the shoreline to work pound nets, and a specialized boat design, the pound boat, was created to serve the fish oil industry. J.S. Darling established a large fish oil factory at the mouth of the Back River in 1879. Menhaden oil was sold to paint and mechanical compound manufacturers. Numerous small marine railways, such as the Darling Marine Railway in Hampton and Smith Railway in Grafton, maintained the various unique boats developed for the seafood industry. This 1912 scene details the deadrise *J.T. Moore* hauled up the Smith's Railway for repairs. Weldon Moore (standing on the deck by the cabin) was later drafted and stationed at Camp Hill in Newport News while serving in the Motor Truck Corps.

Collis P. Huntington's greatest contribution to the Peninsula was almost an afterthought. His new port connected America's heartland with overseas markets, and he realized that many of the ships coming to Newport News for Appalachian coal might require repair. He also recognized that he could build his own ships to carry his coal, which was being delivered by his railroad to his port city. Accordingly, on January 28, 1886, the Chesapeake Dry Dock and Construction Company was chartered to "build and repair steamships, ships, vessels and boats of all dimensions." Huntington owned all of the stock and commenced construction of a dry dock. He intended to build "the best shipyard plant in the world" with "the reputation of building the best ships." On April 24, 1889, the dry dock was officially opened with the docking, at no charge to the Navy, of the monitor *Puritan*. The first ship contract, Hull Number One, was signed in the spring of 1890 to build the tug *Dorothy*. Also that year, the yard's name was changed to the Newport News Shipbuilding and Dry Dock Company. By 1896, the shipyard had been expanded to cover 138 acres along the James River. When the Spanish-American War erupted in 1898, the yard's facilities were able to convert several freighters for the government's use. Depicted in this April 1898 photograph are the hospital ship *Solace*, the USS *Yosemite*, and the USS *Dixie* being readied for service during the Spanish-American War.

The shipyard began bidding on Navy ships in the early 1890s, and in 1893 the yard received contracts to build the gunboats *Nashville*, *Wilmington*, and *Helena*. The double launching of the *Nashville* and *Wilmington* was held on October 19, 1895, the 114th anniversary of the British surrender at Yorktown. All three vessels were delivered to the Navy in 1897. The successful construction of these warships prompted the Navy to award the shipyard with contracts to build the battleships *Kearsarge*, *Kentucky*, *Illinois*, and *Missouri* as well as the monitor *Arkansas*. On March 24, 1898, over 20,000 distinguished spectators witnessed one of the nation's greatest patriotic demonstrations—the launching of the battleships *Kearsarge* and *Kentucky*. A little over a month after this grand event, the U.S. was at war with Spain. The USS *Nashville*, recently completed by the shipyard, fired the war's first shot. America was now an imperialistic power and needed ships to maintain its worldwide presence. The Newport News Shipyard provided many of these new ships, including the USS *Missouri* (pictured above). Admiral George Dewey, a hero of the Spanish-American War, commented that with the *Missouri* at Manila Bay he "could have taken care of the Spanish fleet without further assistance."

The rapid growth of the port, railroad, shipyard, and seafood industry prompted Hampton (1887) and Newport News (1896) to incorporate as cities. Transportation and water systems became important issues to the new cities. Huntington's Old Dominion Land Co. created the Newport News Light and Water Co. The Lee Hall Reservoir was constructed by damming the Warwick River. Road systems also required improvement. The first street railway company was organized in Newport News in 1890 with Colonel Carter M. Braxton as president. "For the present, horses will be used," the April 4, 1891 *Newport News Sun* reported, "but it is expected to abandon them for electricity at an early date." Braxton extended service to Hampton. James S. Darling Jr. established the Hampton and Old Point Railway in 1889, and soon several other trolley lines were completed. This view of downtown Hampton shows streetcar tracks with a trolley approaching in the distance.

By the 1890s, densely populated Newport News had become the center of business on the lower Peninsula. Business districts emerged along several thoroughfares such as Chesnut Avenue (pictured here). Washington Avenue became Newport News's business and entertainment focal point. Large bank buildings, including the First National Bank and Citizen's Marine, soon dotted the streetscape along with department stores, drugstores, and other commercial ventures. The Academy of Music, built in 1900, featured such stars as Al Jolson, Lily Langtry, and George M. Cohan. Movie theaters such as the Nickel Odeon were constructed along the avenue to compete with legitimate theater and vaudeville acts. Other community improvements were rapidly instituted. The city's first telephones were installed in 1898 by the Citizen's Telephone and Telegraph Company. The Library Association was formed in 1891 and amassed over 2,000 volumes.

The new city also needed housing, so Huntington created the Old Dominion Land Company to develop lots 25 feet wide and 100 feet deep. This maximized Huntington's profit and created an orderly town laid on a grid system with numbered streets bisecting two major avenues. Among the first houses built was a row of modest brick structures on Twenty-eighth Street, known as "Quality Row," which contrasted with the frame structures on "Poverty Row." West Avenue, facing the James River, became the desired address for well-to-do residents.

17

As Hampton and Newport News grew into cities, there was a concurrent expansion in the educational systems. By September 1889, 19 schools were providing classes for students. High school-level classes were introduced at Hampton Academy in 1887, but a true high school was not available for students until the West End Academy (later called Hampton High School) opened in 1899. When Hampton Academy burned in 1900, a second high school, Syms-Eaton Academy, was built. The four-room Huntington School, the first school in Newport News, was built by the shipyard in 1888. When the city incorporated in 1896, the school's budget was $13,000, enabling 25 teachers to instruct 833 pupils. The four-story John W. Daniel School, built in 1899 as Central School, served both elementary and secondary schoolchildren.

Efforts were also made to provide higher educational opportunities. Brigadier General Samuel Chapman Armstrong founded the Hampton Normal and Agricultural School in 1888, providing classes for African Americans and Native Americans. Booker T. Washington was one of the school's early students. Dixie Hospital in Hampton opened the Hampton Training School for Nurses in 1892. This photograph shows one of the first graduating classes from the school. The Virginia School for the Deaf and Blind opened in 1905 in Hampton, providing specialized educational opportunities for disabled African Americans.

The C&O Railroad helped foster tourism. The cool sea breezes along the Peninsula's waterfront were now accessible by rail and steamship. Collis P. Huntington had this in mind when his Old Dominion Land Company opened the Hotel Warwick on April 11, 1883. The hotel, overlooking the James River, was Newport News's initial focal point. In 1914, John R. Swinerton, the hotel's first manager, stated the following: "The Hotel Warwick, for several years during the late winter and early spring months, enjoyed the patronage of the best class of tourists from the North, it was kept up to a high standard, the rates being four dollars per day and twenty-one to twenty-five dollars per week—it had as good a chef as could be found and the best that the New York market could supply was none too good for the Warwick . . ."

The Casino Grounds were directly in front of the Hotel Warwick. Originally called Warwick Park, the Old Dominion Land Company created the park to enhance the Hotel Warwick as a tourist attraction as well as to provide recreational opportunities for residents. One advertisement noted how the Hotel Warwick was situated on a bluff overlooking the James River: "Below the bluff stretched a wide sandy bathing beach. Two long piers reached out in the river making this site one of the most active and colorful on the waterfront." The Casino Park included a bandstand, bowling alley, tennis courts, and a pleasure pier. This 1907 photograph highlights a portion of the Casino Grounds and Pier A. The pier stood at the foot of Twenty-eighth Street, and was where steamers docked to unload their passengers and cargo. The steamboats *Pocahontas* and *Hampton* can be seen beside the dock. The *Pocahontas* provided overnight service between Norfolk and Richmond. Pier A was also heavily used by vessels delivering produce to the city until 1915, when Newport News Creek was dredged into a small boat harbor called the Municipal Boat Harbor.

The Peninsula's primary tourist attraction during the 1890s was Old Point Comfort. The original Hygeia Hotel, built just outside of Fort Monroe in 1822, was leveled during the Civil War. A second Hygeia was completed in 1872. Following bankruptcy proceedings in 1873, Harrison Phoebus became the hotel's manager and the Hygeia prospered as one of the nation's leading hotels. One observer noted that "Every room of this big wooden labyrinth has its drowsing occupant, and, sleeping or waking, there are more beauties in the corridors of the Hygeia or along the shaded walks within the fort than one can meet in a decade of travel . . . Perhaps the proximity of Fortress Monroe has not a little to do with the popularity of Old Point Comfort as a health resort." In 1881, the hotel was greatly enlarged and was considered to be "substantially built, lusciously furnished with many of the rooms in suite and fitted with all modern improvements . . . The wide verandas afford spacious and convenient promenades, and during the cold weather over 15,000 square feet of them are encased in glass, enabling the most delicate invalid to enjoy the sunshine and fine water view . . . A spacious pavilion with a floor of 7,000 square feet is set apart for dancing, and choice music is furnished by the United States Artillery School Band throughout the year."

The Hygeia's success prompted the construction of a second grand hotel on Old Point Comfort. An Act of Congress, dated March 3, 1887, authorized John F. Chamberlin, an infamous New York gambler, to construct a hotel across the road leading to the main wharf from the Hygeia. The Chamberlin Hotel was opened to the public on April 4, 1896, and was an instant success. The Hygeia, which had been in a state of decline following the death of Harrison Phoebus in 1888, was razed in 1902. Soon, the Chamberlin became Fort Monroe's social center.

Other resorts were opened in Elizabeth City County near Old Point Comfort. The town of Phoebus (first known as Chesapeake City, later named after Harrison Phoebus) was located across Mill Creek from Fort Monroe and was home to 4 hotels and 52 saloons in 1900. Buckroe Beach was also situated on Chesapeake Bay. In 1897, J.S. Darling's railway company opened the Buckroe Beach Hotel, along with a pavilion and an amusement park. Also in 1897, African-American residents of Hampton constructed the Bay Shore resort near Buckroe, the only Peninsula resort open to African Americans.

The Spanish-American War brought tremendous excitement to the Peninsula. In response to the call for volunteers, members of the Peninsula Guards rallied to the colors. The infantry company, consisting of 87 men from Hampton, Phoebus, and Newport News, left for Richmond on May 20 during a ceremony attended by over 3,000 people. The Peninsula Guards were mustered into service as Company D, 4th Virginia Infantry. The war ended before the unit could embark for Cuba. Company D suffered one death from sickness and returned to the Peninsula in April 1899. The excellent port and rail connections prompted the Army to utilize Newport News as a port of embarkation. Campgrounds were laid out next to the C&O terminal on the Casino Grounds and in a field between Thirty-fourth and Thirty-sixth Streets, next to the shipyard. Local members of the Huntington Rifles guarded the waterfront from possible attack by the Spanish fleet while troops assembled for embarkation. The camps closed as soon as the war ended.

The Spanish-American War revealed the weak defenses of Hampton Roads. Efforts were made afterwards to complete improvements designed by the Endicott Board to Fort Monroe and Fort Wool. The board, organized in 1886 by Secretary of War William C. Endicott, developed a new system of coastal defense to update the Civil War-era forts that protected major harbors.

The Endicott System at Fort Monroe was comprised of a series of detached massive batteries constructed outside the old masonry fort. Each battery was specifically designed for 10-inch and 12-inch disappearing guns or 12-inch mortars. Smaller batteries were designed to mount 6-inch disappearing guns and 3-inch rapid fire guns. The batteries were constructed of reinforced concrete covered by thick earthen parapets. Seven batteries, including Battery Eustis (pictured here), were eventually built to enable Fort Monroe to continue protecting the entrance to the Chesapeake Bay and Hampton Roads.

Two

PRELUDE TO WAR

When the *Daily Press* reported that war had erupted between the European powers in August 1914, few Peninsula residents seemed concerned about the distant conflict. Citizens generally agreed with the 1914 Thanksgiving Day *Daily Press* editorial, which stated that "While Europe is in the throes of war, with famine staring many in the face, we have peace and plenty, and the smile of a beneficent Providence is upon us." This image depicts a training exercise at Fort Monroe in 1914. Few Army leaders, however, considered the possibility that the nation would ever become embroiled in the European War.

Regardless of how much the local community wished to avoid involvement in the European conflict, economic realities quickly brought the war to the Peninsula's doorstep. Newport News was a major seaport connecting the heartland of the nation with overseas markets. European nations, particularly the Allies, sought food and other goods necessary to maintain their war effort. The waterfront soon hummed with activity and the Peninsula began its wartime boom. The remount station, depicted in this photograph with William Pettit and George Rowan in the Model T, was one of the first efforts to transport war material from the Peninsula to Europe.

Shortly after the war began, the British Army established a remount station in Newport News to ship horses and mules to Great Britain. Commanded by Captain James Gregg, the operation was so successful that it was soon expanded, forwarding vast quantities of grain and other commodities through the port's terminals. Newport News would eventually be remembered as the port that sent 457,000 animals overseas to the Allied Powers.

Several Newport News firms profited from trade with the belligerent nations. The Waterfront Lumber Company, located on Eighteenth Street, received a contract to recondition ship stalls damaged by livestock. Discarded lumber would remain for many years after the war outside the company's shop. Employment opportunities grew as trade increased. This image of the remount station's "Blacksmith Gang" depicts several of the men completing war work for the Allies.

The war came closer to the Peninsula in 1914, when several vessels of the Central Powers sought temporary refuge at Hampton Roads. The first ships to arrive were the Austro-Hungarian steamship *Budapest*, which weighed nearly 5,500 tons, and the *Arcadia*, a German liner bound for New Orleans with a cargo of toys. These vessels chose to be interned along Newport News's Thirty-first Street pier rather than risk capture by the Royal Navy.

In the spring of 1915, Newport News received two more dramatic arrivals. The German commerce raiders *Eitel Friedrich* and *Kronprinz Wilhelm* slipped past British patrols seeking the cruisers and entered Hampton Roads. The raiders docked at the shipyard for fuel and repairs but lingered in port beyond the time limit set by international law. The captains of both vessels elected to be interned rather than risk capture by four British warships waiting for them outside the Chesapeake Capes.

The *Eitel Friedrich* and *Kronprinz Wilhelm* had already served their nation well before being interned. The *Eitel Friedrich* alone captured 11 prizes in its spectacular cruise across the Pacific Ocean and around Cape Horn. This commerce raider left China on August 6, 1914, and was considered a ghost ship by British authorities until she sought sanctuary at Newport News on March 10, 1915. The *Eitel Friedrich* had on board 23 American sailors from the four-masted steel bark *William Frye*. The *William Frye* was sunk on January 27, 1915, in the South Atlantic. This was Imperial Germany's first overt act of war against the U.S.

The *Eitel Friedrich* and the *Kronprinz Wilhelm* became tourist attractions for curiosity seekers striving to learn more about the German war effort. The ships were eventually transferred to Portsmouth, where crew members established a miniature "German village" at the Gosport Naval Shipyard until they were made POWs when the U.S. declared war on Germany. The federal government transformed the vessels into the troop carriers *DeKalb* (the *Eitel Friedrich*) and *Von Steuben* (the *Kronprinz Wilhelm*). The *Budapest* and the *Arcadia* remained at Newport News until they, too, were pressed into service. Two crewmen became permanent residents of Newport News—E. Smola, the first officer of the *Budapest*, opened a nautical instruments company, and carpenter Carl Kruse of the *Arcadia* became a resident of Hilton Village.

The arrival of the RMS *Appam* on January 31, 1916, prompted even greater excitement along the Newport News waterfront. The *Appam* was captured while on a voyage from South Africa to Liverpool by the German commerce raider *Moewe*. It was brought into Hampton Roads by a 23-man prize crew after its 3,000-mile voyage. The ship anchored just off the Casino Grounds. Many of the British citizens on board, headed by Lord and Lady Merriweather, were relieved to arrive in American waters. Their first expressed wish was for a "cup of tea," so they were immediately escorted to the Hotel Warwick for such refreshment. The *Appam* remained at Newport News for over a year. The British and African Steam Navigation Co., Ltd., filed a lawsuit to reclaim the ship. The case ultimately went to the U.S. Supreme Court, which in March 1917 decided on behalf of the ship's owners, and the *Appam* was released.

The German U-Boat and commerce raider campaign against Great Britain eventually embroiled the U.S. in the war. The one event that made the U-Boat terror very real to Americans was the May 7, 1915 sinking of the Cunard liner *Lusitania* off the coast of Ireland. Over a thousand lives were lost. Among the 124 Americans who perished was shipyard president Albert L. Hopkins. Hopkins was traveling to Europe with shipyard treasurer Fred J. Gauntlett to obtain contracts from the Allies. Gauntlett somehow survived by swimming to safety. (He would often recount his story until his death in 1951.) When news of Hopkins's death reached Newport News, the yard was closed for a half day in his honor. Americans were outraged over the *Lusitania*'s sinking. The rallying cry of "Remember the *Lusitania*" had special meaning for Peninsula residents and helped to turn public opinion against Germany.

On July 22, 1915, Homer Lenior Ferguson was named president of Newport News Shipbuilding. Ferguson, a U.S. Naval Academy graduate from North Carolina, resigned from the Navy in 1904 to work at the shipyard. He was promoted to general superintendent in 1911 and assumed the position of general manager in 1912. Ferguson's entire family gathered together for this 1918 photograph. Pictured, from left to right, are Charles, Isabel, Elise, Mrs. Ferguson, Homer L. Ferguson, Walter, William, and Homer Jr.

Ferguson had already been busy improving morale at the yard. He converted a building at the corner of Madison Avenue and Twenty-third Street for use as a YMCA for African-American shipyard workers. He also established a safety plan, an employee suggestion plan, a medical department, and a retirement allowance plan, all of which were needed as the yard's work force rapidly increased. In 1917, over 7,000 workers were employed, a figure which increased to 12,500 by 1919. In this 1917 photograph, riveters are hard at work on another vessel.

Ferguson also began preparing the yard in the eventuality of American involvement in the war. In January 1916, $400,000 in plant improvements were initiated.

The Newport News Shipbuilding and Dry Dock Co. forged a reputation for building quality ships for the Navy. Before the U.S. entered World War I, the shipyard had constructed eight submarines (three for the Navy) and several battleships, including the USS *Pennsylvania*. The *Pennsylvania*, pictured here, was launched in 1915 and commissioned on June 12, 1916.

A new town was born in 1916 on the Peninsula. The town of Penniman, named for Russell S. Penniman, the inventor of ammonia dynamite, was established in York County. It was developed by the E.I. DuPont Company along the York River, between Queens and King Creeks. DuPont required a new plant for manufacturing artillery shells to meet the Allied demand for ammunition. The industrial village of Penniman had its own churches, restaurants, post office, hotel, hospital, YMCA, school, and police force.

Three

DEFENDING
HAMPTON ROADS

The Spanish-American War made it very evident that the defense of Hampton Roads was inadequate and required modernization. Even though work had begun on Endicott improvements to Fort Monroe, they were still incomplete in 1898. Battery Irwin, pictured here c. 1910, was built to emplace four rapid-fire guns overlooking the main channel directly opposite Fort Wool.

Only two batteries were completed by the outbreak of the Spanish-American War. Battery Bomford, a two-gun battery for 10-inch Model 1888 M-II guns mounted on Buffington-Crozier disappearing carriages, cost $154,379.99 and was completed in 1897. Disappearing carriages worked on a pair of massive lever arms that enabled the gun's recoil to return the gun to a protected position. The 10-inch rifle had a maximum range of 12,259 yards and could fire two rounds per minute.

This massive concrete redoubt, finished in 1899, contained four in-line pits housing sixteen 12-inch Model 1890 M-I mortars, which had a maximum range of almost 15,000 yards. The redoubt was divided into two batteries, Battery Anderson and Battery Ruggles.

After 1900, major Congressional appropriations funded the remainder of Fort Monroe's armament improvements. This modernization effort included the rapid gun emplacements atop the old fort and additional concrete batteries to house disappearing guns. The Old Water battery was removed to permit the construction of Battery Parrott. Battery Parrott mounted 12-inch disappearing rifles, by far the most powerful weapons ever emplaced on Fort Monroe. The 12-inch rifles weighed 59 tons and had a range of 17,000 yards. The modernization was complete by 1910 and included several other batteries, such as Bomford, Eustis, DeRussy, Church, and Montgomery.

Fort Wool, located on the RipRaps in the middle of the entrance to Hampton Roads, was also modernized during the early 1900s. A total of five batteries were constructed atop the unfinished Civil War-era fort. Battery Henry Lee, designed for four 15-pounder guns, was the first gun emplacement completed. Another two 15-pounder gun battery, named Battery Jacob Hindman, was built shortly thereafter in 1903. The construction of Batteries Ferdinand Claiborne, Alexander Dyer, and Horatio Gates completed Fort Wool's modernization. These batteries, including Battery Ferdinand Claiborne, pictured here with Mathews and Gloucester National Guardsmen in 1917, mounted 6-inch disappearing guns.

33

Fort Monroe's Artillery School was significantly upgraded during this era. The fort's old arsenal building was remodeled to serve as a classroom and laboratory. The school was closed during the Spanish-American War and reopened in 1900. The Army's experience during the Spanish-American War prompted a wide variety of reforms. The Artillery Corps was divided in 1907 to form the Field Artillery and the Coast Artillery Corps. Consequently, Fort Monroe's Artillery School was transformed into the Coast Artillery School. The school was combined with the School of Submarine Defense and opened on September 1, 1908. This expansion of the Coast Artillery School required additional housing and classroom space. Construction of new academic buildings, quarters, and a library began in 1909 and was completed by 1912.

Fort Monroe was the center for training all Coast Artillery Corps personnel and developing new material for seacoast defense. The fort also served as the headquarters of one of the strongest harbor defense systems in North America. When the U.S. entered World War I, Fort Monroe immediately became the nerve center for the region's defense. Fort Wool was garrisoned and additional seacoast guns were mounted on Cape Henry (Fort Story) and Fisherman Island (Fort Custis) to defend the mouth of the Chesapeake Bay. A submarine net and mine defenses were laid to help protect the entrance to Hampton Roads harbor.

The Coast Artillery School was expanded during World War I as Fort Monroe became the headquarters of the Coast Artillery Training Center. A series of officer candidate training camps were held at Fort Monroe to prepare officers for harbor defense and heavy artillery service. The first camp processed 1,277 candidates with courses ranging from mortars and field fortifications to signaling and administration.

Fort Monroe was overflowing as a result of the ever increasing influx of instructors, officer candidates, enlisted personnel, and coast artillery units. The construction of 40 cantonment-style buildings began in 1917; eventually, over 250 buildings, some completed in less than three weeks, were built on Fort Monroe during World War I. The post began to expand north along the beach toward Buckroe Beach. A fill was started with temporary bulkheads along the shores of Mill Creek. The shoreline west of the fort was also filled, and buildings were erected for the use of the Coast Artillery School Department of Enlisted Specialists.

Despite all of the efforts to expand Fort Monroe's capacity, more space was required, so the Army decided to establish a larger artillery training area in upper Warwick County. Camp Eustis was built on Mulberry Island, which had been purchased from various landowners for the total cost of $538,000. Over 200 families were displaced in the process. Mulberry Island was

chosen because French military advisors believed that a firing range featuring terrain obstacles would better prepare the American artillerists for trench warfare on the Western Front. Because Camp Eustis only provided a 7,000-yard range, Camp Wallace was later established near Grove Wharf. This second camp enabled the practice range to be increased to 20,000 yards.

The construction of Camp Eustis began on April 28, 1918. Headquarters Company and Battery A, 2nd Trench Mortar Battalion, were detached from Fort Monroe to provide administration and military police, and to initiate the fabrication of target trenches. Batteries C and D, 81st Artillery, were the first troops to occupy the camp in late May 1918. Camp Eustis's building program was completed at such a rapid pace that, by the end of August 1918, the camp could accommodate 19,000 men.

Camp Eustis became the concentration point and training area for heavy artillery units destined for embarkation overseas. Over 20,000 men passed through the camp during the war. Since the camp's primary purpose was to house several schools, it soon became known as the "experimental shop of the Coast Artillery." Schools provided training in trench mortars and motor transport. Two new fields of artillery science, anti-aircraft and railway artillery, were pioneered on Camp Eustis. The vast marshes of Mulberry Island were perfect for firing heaving artillery, and some exercises were completed under simulated combat conditions.

The Peninsula Guards were disbanded following the Spanish-American War. Many Hampton community leaders, however, recognized that events in Mexico and Europe hinted the possibility of a future conflict and sought to rekindle the Peninsula's citizen soldier spirit by organizing a field artillery battery. Battery D, 1st Virginia Field Artillery, was established on November 19, 1915. The unit mustered five officers and 133 enlisted men. Hampton lawyer Thornton F. Jones, pictured here, joined the Virginia National Guard on November 9, 1915. Jones was later promoted to captain on August 4, 1917, and assumed command of Battery D until honorably discharged on January 21, 1918, due to medical reasons.

Battery D ~ 1st Virginia Field Artillery ~ Hampton, Va. Assembled to depart for the front ~ June 27, 1916.

An armory was secured for Battery D when the Newport News and Hampton Railway Gas and Electric Co. provided buildings on Sunset Creek. Drilling began and the battery received its first shipment of artillery horses in January 1916. When Pancho Villa raided Columbus, New Mexico, on March 9, 1916, the National Guard was mobilized and Battery D was mustered into federal service at Camp Stuart in Richmond. Even though the men had not received their uniforms, a grand parade was held in Hampton on June 27, 1916. Battery D was now off to war.

On October 2, 1916, the battery entrained at Richmond for Camp Wilson in San Antonio, Texas. It received its full compliment of horses, caissons, and artillery while training at Camp Wilson. This photograph depicts the 4th Section, Battery D, training in Texas.

Even though this photograph shows Lieutenant Thornton Jones and two other members of Battery D apparently enjoying themselves, a majority of the soldiers found the Texas winter depressing. They spent their time fighting mud rather than Mexicans.

On November 2, 1916, Battery D began a 25-mile march to Leon Springs, Texas. The battery trained at Leon Springs for six weeks before returning to Camp Wilson. By this time, Brigadier General John J. Pershing's Mexican Punitive Expedition ended, and on March 11, 1917, Battery D returned to Hampton.

Battery D was enthusiastically welcomed home. The citizenry insisted that the battery parade through the streets of Hampton en route to its armory on Sunset Creek. On March 14, 1917, Battery D was mustered out of federal service.

Four

INTO THE
WILD BLUE YONDER

World War I was the first war in which aviation played a major battlefield role. Warfare on the Western Front had clearly demonstrated to American observers that air power was a critical component of a modern army. Government and civilian leaders sought to prepare the U.S. for entry into the war as an Allied Power and the Peninsula quickly became one of the nation's centers for aerial training.

The Peninsula had already made a name for itself in aviation history when, on November 10, 1910, pilot Eugene B. Ely became the first person to launch an airplane from a warship. Ely's 4-cylinder engine Curtiss pusher biplane took off from the cruiser *Birmingham* in Hampton Roads. The plane touched water briefly, but Ely landed his plane safely on Willoughby Spit. Two months later, Ely performed the even more difficult feat of landing on a wooden platform built atop the deck of the USS *Pennsylvania* in San Francisco Bay.

Five years after Eugene Ely's epic feat, Glenn Hammond Curtiss decided to open a branch of his civilian flying school on the Peninsula. An aviation pioneer whose contribution to the history of flight in the U.S. was exceeded only by that of the Wright Brothers, Curtis began his career similar to the Wrights, building motors for bicycles. His obsession with speed and engines led him into the field of motorcycle racing. When he was not breaking motorcycle speed records, his thoughts turned to aviation. In 1904, Curtiss received a contract to build a lightweight motor for Thomas Baldwin's dirigible *California Arrow*, which lead to his building the motor for the U.S. Army's first dirigible. In October 1907, Curtiss formed the Aerial Experiment Association with Alexander Graham Bell and began making airplanes. His most famous aircraft was the Curtiss Jenny (pictured here at the Curtiss Flying School).

The third plane Curtiss built, the June Bug, made aviation history. He won the Scientific American Trophy in 1908 for the first mile-long public flight, during which his plane reached a speed of "almost 40 miles per hour." Then, on May 31, 1910, he won the trophy for a third time with a spectacular flight down the Hudson River from Albany to New York. His greatest feat, however, took place in January 1911 when, in a plane equipped with pontoons, he took off from and landed on water in San Diego harbor. He subsequently received the first contract to build planes for the U.S. Navy.

Late in 1910, Curtiss established his first flight training school near San Diego, California. He then decided to expand his operations to a warm location on the East Coast. Curtiss selected Newport News as the site for his training center and organized the school in 1915. Captain Thomas Scott Baldwin, a balloonist who is also credited with making the first parachute jump, was placed in command of the school. Baldwin is pictured here in civilian clothes with several of the school's instructors.

Curtiss selected a flat, 20-acre track next to the Newport News Small Boat Harbor for his school. The location provided railroad and steamship access, and enabled him to complete further seaplane experiments and training with the U.S. Navy Base across Hampton Roads.

The Small Boat Harbor was built from the watercourse once known as Captain Tucker's Creek and Newport News Creek. Dredging operations and other improvements, completed in 1915, made the municipal harbor 300 feet wide and 1,400 feet long.

The Curtiss Flying School offered a 400-minute course of instruction at the cost of $1 a minute. Despite the expense, the school proved to be a tremendous success. Individuals keen on learning how to fly throughout America and as far as Canada, Italy, France, and Sweden were attracted to the school. The first class at the Curtiss Flying School was composed primarily of Canadians. These Royal Flying Corps volunteers were anxious to serve overseas and did not want to wait for a place in an official school.

Several illustrious Americans came to Newport News to obtain their Aero Club of America license at the Curtiss Flying School. "In order to get your certificate," Louis Fediler stated, "you had to be able to fly three figure eights around two pylons." Vernon Castle, the famous ballroom dancer, traveled from New York to attend classes. Castle maintained rooms at the Chamberlin Hotel during his instruction. Another famous student was Geoffrey O'Hara, who was the composer of the popular rag-time hit "K-K-K-Katie."

Some of the leading figures in American aviation, such as Eddie Rickenbacker, were associated with the flying school. Instructors Eddie Stinson and Victor Carlstrom were record-breaking aviators. Colonel Billy Mitchell traveled by train each weekend from Washington, D.C., to earn his wings. On his first solo flight, he flipped the plane over. The first local graduate was H.M. "Buck" Gallop. Gallop went on to become an ace in France. Legend persists that actor Richard Bathelmess modeled his character in the 1930 Oscar-winning film *The Dawn Patrol* on Gallop's career.

The Curtiss Flying School became a popular local attraction. Sightseers flocked to the Small Boat Harbor each weekend to watch the skies for the next aerial acrobatic feat. Pilots dazzled the crowds with astonishing loop the loops, speed records, and other daring stunts.

The stunts and training sometimes resulted in disaster. Student David Alvord almost collided with a trolley car while flying low over Jefferson Avenue. He swerved just in time to miss the trolley, but crashed instead into a restaurant, with his propeller coming to rest on a lunch counter. Fortunately, no one was hurt. Other accidents were more serious. Instructor Steven McGordon was badly burned and later died after his Curtiss Jenny crashed. Victor Carlstrom, chief instructor, and student Cary B. Epes of Newport News were killed on May 9, 1917, when the right wing of their plane collapsed during a training flight.

The Army assumed operation of the Curtiss Flying School in 1917. The school then became known as the Atlantic Coast Aeronautical Station. Even though the station evolved into a center for testing experimental aircraft, competition from other schools limited the number of available students. The Navy opened an aviation institute on the old Jamestown Expedition site in Norfolk, which would eventually become the Oceana Naval Air Station. Also in 1917, Langley Field opened in Hampton. Langley Field provided the Army with a large air field as well as schools for aerial observation and photography.

Once the war ended, the Curtiss Flying School remained in operation for only a few more years. Besides the competition for students from nearby military aviation schools, the Small Boat Harbor provided little room for expansion. An alternate location was sought in Norfolk and Buckroe Beach, but these efforts failed. The Curtiss Flying School closed in 1922.

Hampton also became an aviation center during World War I. Congress established the National Advisory Committee for Aeronautics (NACA) on March 3, 1915, to continue the aeronautical studies begun by Samuel Pierpont Langley, former secretary of the Smithsonian Institution. The NACA teamed with the Army and Navy to procure land on which to create a facility dedicated to aviation research and experimentation. The Army Appropriation Act of 1916 provided the funds; however, a site in the Chesapeake Bay region needed to be identified. Three Hamptonians, Harry H. Holt, H.R. Booker, and Nelson S. Groome, organized a citizen's committee and purchased 1,659.4 acres to offer the federal government. The property included the Sherwood, Lamington, Tide Mill, and Downing Farms. The Newport News-Hampton Railway Gas and Electric Co. offered trolley service that included a bridge wide enough for automobile traffic, while the Newport News Light and Water Co. offered to supply water. On December 5, 1916, after several months of investigation, the NACA purchased the Back River site for $290,000. The Langley Field surveying crew is depicted in this 1917 photograph.

The Back River site was exactly what the NACA wanted. It was near an existing military installation and industry and in a temperate climate. Furthermore, the land was suitable for landing and take-off as well as over-water flying. The headquarters of the Aviation Experimental Station and Proving Grounds opened in downtown Hampton in February 1917, but construction of the base did not begin until two months later. On August 7, 1917, the base was officially named Langley Field, in honor of Samuel Pierpont Langley.

Even before construction was completed, units began to arrive at Langley Field. The 5th Aviation School Squadron was formed in June 1917. This unit, later designated the 119th Aero Squadron and the Detachment 11, Air Service, Air Production, was the only detachment available to test the wide variety of American and foreign aircraft arriving at Langley Field for evaluation. Airplanes like the Albree Monoplane, the Thomas Morse S-4 Scout, the Macchi M-5 Flying Boat, the Bristol Fighter, and the Caproni CA-33 were evaluated for possible U.S. Air Service use. This photograph depicts a Curtiss JN-4 Jenny over Langley Field. The Jenny was the workhorse for pilot training at Langley.

The U.S. Army School of Aerial Photography was established in October 1917 at Langley Field. Sergeant M.A. McKinney, later promoted to captain, was placed in command of the school. McKinney, with assistance provided by foreign personnel such as Sergeant Major C.O. Hasslet of the Royal Flying Corps, organized the new school. It included a pilot school, a school of photographers and observers, and a photo detachment. The first class of 12 "aero photographers" graduated in January 1918 and was immediately sent to France.

In March 1918, the U.S. Army School of Aerial Observers was organized at Langley Field. The School of Aerial Photography, however, was soon transferred to Rochester, New York. One component of the original School of Aerial Photography, the School of Aerial Photographic Reconnaissance, which provided the final training, remained at Langley. The School of Aerial Observers was redesignated as the Air Service Flying School. It disbanded in November 1919. This photograph depicts soldiers installing an aerial camera on a Curtiss Jenny.

Construction delays in the completion of Langley Field prompted the Army to shift many aviation experimental activities to McCook Field (later renamed Wright Field) in Dayton, Ohio. Langley, however, retained responsibility for bombing, photography, radio, and telegraph experiments. Units serving at Langley consequently developed an improved compass, a turn

indicator, recognition lights for aircraft, and a new gunsight. The Army also endeavored to increase the airfield contingent at Langley Field in 1918. By the war's end, 10 aero squadrons, 15 construction companies, and 1 balloon detachment were stationed at Langley.

Langley Field was slated to play a larger role in the aviation war effort, but the numerous problems encountered building the base precluded greater use. Langley became known as "the bottleneck of the aircraft program." Much of the delays could be blamed on the Back River marshlands selected for Langley Field; one of the workers noted that the new air field had "the muddiest mud, the weediest weeds, the dustiest dust, and the most ferocious mosquitoes the world has ever known." The war department eventually assumed the responsibility for completing the project with the intent to make "Langley Field . . . one of the prettiest, as well as best equipped, flying experimental stations in the country." Work was nearly completed on housing and other base facilities by the war's end. This photograph depicts members of the 5th Aviation School Squadron in front of the old Sherwood Cottage, which was used as quarters until barracks were erected.

Besides fixed-wing aircraft, the Army also used balloons and airships during World War I. Two balloon companies, the 10th and 19th Balloon Companies, were stationed at Langley Field. These units utilized free balloons; however, one non-rigid A-4 airship was deployed at Langley. Observation balloons were considered a useful method of gathering tactical information. The Army accordingly established the Lee Hall Balloon School at Camp Eustis in 1918.

The Imperial German Air Service popularized the use of balloons and zeppelins during the early portion of the war. Zeppelins were used to bomb targets in Great Britain; however, they proved to be very vulnerable to anti-aircraft and fixed-wing aircraft fire. Since the U.S. Army did not have a balloon service before the war, there was an acute shortage of men and equipment to undertake the mission of the U.S. Air Service Balloon Section—to regulate artillery fire, to locate targets, and to report all activity within the enemy lines. Consequently, the Lee Hall Balloon School was established to provide specialized training for aerial observation work in gas balloons. The school focused on artillery support observation work as well as the operation of balloon winches, telephone line work, look-out work, machine gunnery, and radio operation. The Army considered it imperative to utilize gas observation balloons during the war and the Lee Hall Balloon School became one of the major ballon training facilities in the U.S. The typical U.S. Army gas balloon, as seen in this 1918 photograph, was designed with a gondola at the balloon's stern to carry two men to a height of about 2,000 feet. The balloons were attached to the ground by cables, and if attacked, they could be quickly winched back to the ground. This design and system enabled balloons to provide an important battlefield link between forward observation intelligence and artillery.

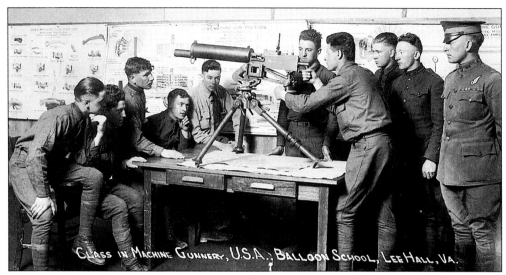

Class in Machine Gunnery, U.S.A.; Balloon School, Lee Hall, Va.

The Lee Hall Balloon School was constructed at a cost of $1,5 million and had a capacity of 1,442 students. The school's presence at Camp Eustis provided an excellent opportunity for balloon training in conjunction with heavy artillery target practice. As many as seven balloons could be lofted simultaneously to observe artillery testing. The Lee Hall Balloon School was unique in that it was the only Army balloon school that combined both land and water observation training.

Commanding Officer and Adjutant, U.S.A. Balloon School, Lee Hall, Va.

By 1920, the Lee Hall Balloon School was one of only three similar Army schools. The school's post-war commander was a balloon veteran and winner of the Distinguished Service Medal, Lieutenant Colonel John A. Paegelow. Like the Curtiss Flying School, the Lee Hall Balloon School closed in the 1920s. Nevertheless, these schools with the experimental activities at Langley Field enabled the Peninsula to play a major role in the development and training of the Army Air Service during World War I.

Five

HAMPTON ROADS PORT OF EMBARKATION

The Peninsula was already engaged in wartime work when President Woodrow Wilson asked Congress to declare war against Germany on April 6, 1917. Local military bases, shipyards, air fields, ports, and people turned their focus toward the nation's crusade to make the world safe for democracy. Wilson actually visited the Peninsula several times during his presidency, as depicted in this city street view of Newport News. His daughter Margaret twice sang for troops stationed at Camp Hill. The YMCA hut at Camp Stuart was dedicated in her honor.

LOADING A MULL
ABOARD U.S. ARMY
TRANSPORT AT
NEWPORT NEWS, VA

The Army, in anticipation of America's entry into the war, surveyed the Hampton Roads area in early 1917 to ascertain where to establish a port of embarkation. Newport News was selected over Norfolk as headquarters for the Hampton Roads Port of Embarkation in July 1917.

It was said that Newport News was chosen as the Hampton Roads Port of Embarkation's headquarters "solely on the industry of her people." There were, however, many other geographical factors that influenced the decision. Norfolk was a congested port and already the center for many naval activities. Newport News offered good port facilities, a large harbor, excellent railroad connections, and an abundance of available land. The Army assumed operations of the port from the C&O in July 1918 and immediately began the construction of embarkation camps.

Even though Hampton Roads was well fortified by Fort Monroe and other coastal defense installations defending the lower Chesapeake Bay, the Peninsula was in an uproar on July 5, 1917, over the rumored appearance of a German submarine in the bay. Battery D, which had been called back into Federal Service on April 2, 1917, was already encamped on the Casino Grounds in downtown Newport News to defend the port. The battery pictured here remained in Newport News until August, when troops left for training at Camp McClellan, Alabama. A submarine net was laid between Fort Monroe and Fort Wool to block any possible U-Boat excursions. Virginia pilot Captain Nelson Smith remembered that "minesweepers would clear a path by pulling a long metallic thing behind them to detonate mines" that might have been deposited by an enemy submarine.

Every precaution available to protect transports leaving Hampton Roads was considered prudent. After all, the Hampton Roads Port of Embarkation was one of only two (New York City was the other) military ports created to ship doughboys overseas. In less than two years, 145 transports moved 261,820 soldiers from Newport News to France.

Colonel Grote Hutchinson, later a brigadier general, was named commander of the port. He established the Hampton Roads Port of Embarkation's headquarters in the Federal Building in downtown Newport News. Camps were also needed in the outlying countryside to station men prior to shipment overseas. Thus, the Army acquired large tracts of property in Warwick

County from the Old Dominion Land Company to build five troop cantonments. Camp Stuart, pictured here, was named in honor of Confederate cavalry general J.E.B. Stuart. It was the first and largest camp to be built.

Camp Stuart was constructed on a 309-acre tract overlooking Hampton Roads between Ivy Avenue and Salter's Creek. It was the Army's largest embarkation camp during the war. Almost 115,000 doughboys passed through Camp Stuart en route to Europe. The camp was hastily built between July and December 1917 and consisted of row after row of barracks, mess halls, and other support structures, including a huge 50-ward hospital.

Camp Hill was constructed simultaneously with Camp Stuart. It was also a very large installation covering acreage along the James River from Sixty-fourth Street to Newport News's Huntington Park. The combined cost of these two camps reached nearly $16 million.

Like Camp Stuart, Camp Hill was also named for a Confederate general, Lieutenant General Ambrose Powell Hill. The camp sent 63,887 men overseas. Many military camps, bases, and forts throughout the South were named in honor of Confederate generals and other Southern heroes. Fort Hood (John Bell Hood) in Texas and Fort Bragg (Braxton Bragg) in North Carolina follow this tradition, which was instituted by the Army to alleviate any lingering bitterness in the South remaining from the Civil War and the Reconstruction era.

MOTOR TRUCK CAMP CAP
CAMP HILL.
SEPT. 28

While Camp Hill served as the port's center for the Motor Truck Corps, it played an even greater role as the animal embarkation area. Camp Hill's large veterinary hospital and livestock pen required 900 men to care for the horses and mules. The camp's capacity was 10,000 animals.

A total of 33,704 horses and 24,474 mules were shipped overseas through the camp. These animals consumed the following amount of feed: 82,870,000 pounds of hay, 41,392,000 pounds of oats, and 7,273,000 pounds of bran.

The vast quantities of animals and supplies processed through the port prompted the Army to billet several African-American stevedore and labor battalions at Camp Hill. This circumstance resulted in several incidents between black and white soldiers. In particular, the quarters provided for African-American soldiers proved to be inadequate. They suffered terribly during the 1917–18 winter, with as many as 20 to 30 men assigned to a tent. There were few blankets, heat was provided by open fires, and the food was served outdoors.

The Army sought to correct this problem and constructed Camp Alexander to house African-American labor battalions. Named in honor of one of the first African-American West Point graduates, Lieutenant John Hanks Alexander of the 9th U.S. Cavalry, the camp was completed in August 1918 and formed the northern portion of Camp Hill along the C&O tracks. A total of 57,081 African Americans embarked for France from Camp Alexander.

An Air Service depot was organized along the C&O tracks in the Gum Grove section of Warwick County. The 295-acre site was named for Colonel J.S. Morrison, construction engineer of the Peninsula Division of the C&O Railroad.

Camp Morrison served as the embarkation center for balloon units and aero squadrons. Over 10,000 men were processed through Camp Morrison en route to France. The camp included 24 warehouses built for the storage of aviation equipment and supplies.

Christmas Dinner, 1918

Quartermaster Detachment

The Smith family provided their antebellum estate, Cedar Grove, for use by the officers of nearby Camp Morrison. The family stayed in Newport News while the officers, according to Nelson Smith, "liked to have wrecked the place."

The entire Peninsula was teaming with troops by summer 1918. Camp Stuart became the largest embarkation camp, both in size and number of troops processed, in the U.S. In August 1918, a total of 46,130 men left Newport News aboard 31 vessels bound for France. Initially, the soldiers marched to their transports at night in order to avoid information leaks. Such secrecy was soon deemed unnecessary and units marched in grand parades, complete with bands playing martial music, to the piers. This photograph is a view of Camp Morrison's band in July 1918.

Thomas Wolfe, a worker at both Langley Field and the Newport News Shipyard, wrote about the endless movement of troops in his book *Look Homeward Angel:* "Twice a week the troops went through. They stood densely in brown and weary thousands on the pier while a council of officers, tabled at the gang ways, went through their clearance papers. Then, each below the sweating torture of his pack, they were filed from the hot furnace of the pier into the hotter prison of the ship. The great ships, with their motley jagged patches of deception, waited in the stream; they slid in and out in unending squadrons."

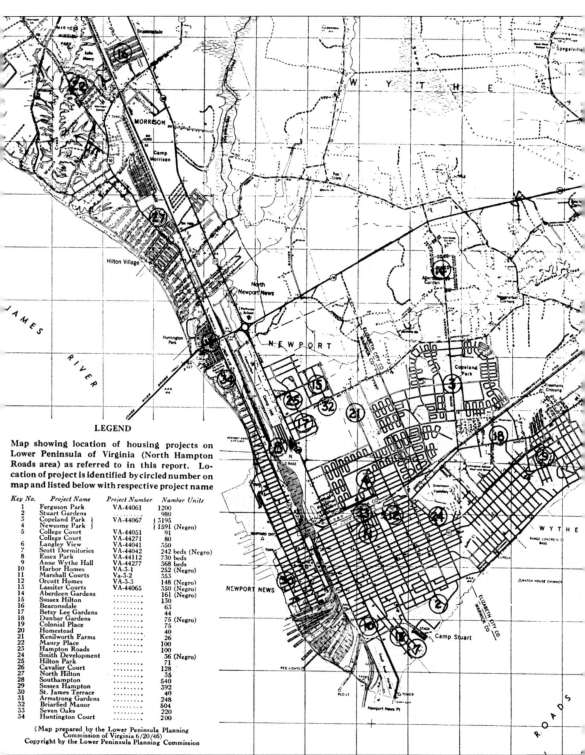

LEGEND

Map showing location of housing projects on Lower Peninsula of Virginia (North Hampton Roads area) as referred to in this report. Location of project is identified by circled number on map and listed below with respective project name

Key No.	Project Name	Project Number	Number Units
1	Ferguson Park	VA-44061	1200
2	Stuart Gardens	....	980
3	Copeland Park }	VA-44067	{ 3195
4	Newsome Park }		{ 1591 (Negro)
5	College Court	VA-44051	91
	College Court	VA-44271	80
6	Langley View	VA-44041	550
7	Scott Dormitories	VA-44042	242 beds (Negro)
8	Essex Park	VA-44112	730 beds
9	Anne Wythe Hall	VA-44277	368 beds
10	Harbor Homes	VA-3-1	252 (Negro)
11	Marshall Courts	Va-3-2	353
12	Orcutt Homes	VA-3-3	148 (Negro)
13	Lassiter Courts	VA-44065	350 (Negro)
14	Aberdeen Gardens	....	161 (Negro)
15	Sussex Hilton	....	130
16	Beaconsdale	....	63
17	Betsy Lee Gardens	....	44
18	Dunbar Gardens	....	75 (Negro)
19	Colonial Place	....	75
20	Homestead	....	40
21	Kenilworth Farms	....	26
22	Maury Place	....	100
23	Hampton Roads	....	100
24	Smith Development	....	36 (Negro)
25	Hilton Park	....	71
26	Cavalier Court	....	128
27	North Hilton	....	35
28	Southampton	....	540
29	Sussex Hampton	....	392
30	St. James Terrace	....	40
31	Armstrong Gardens	....	248
32	Briarfied Manor	....	504
33	Seven Oaks	....	220
34	Huntington Court	....	200

(Map prepared by the Lower Peninsula Planning Commission of Virginia 6/20/46)
Copyright by the Lower Peninsula Planning Commission

This map of the lower Peninsula details the excellent port facilities, military installations (Fort Monroe, Fort Wool, and Langley Field) and several of the World War I Hampton Roads Port of

Embarkation camps (Camp Stuart, Camp Hill, Camp Alexander, and Camp Morrison).

Private Herbert G. Smith, later a Newport News judge, vividly remembered the arduous march from Camp Hill to the C&O piers. Smith said that it was "the hottest day I ever saw in my life. My colonel knew I was from Newport News and asked me when we got to Washington Avenue and Twenty-eighth Street, how much further it was. I said, 'You just as well to keep walking now, we're almost there.' " Instead, the commander stopped his regiment for a brief rest, and Smith recounted that he "laid down on the street car tracks right in the middle of Washington Avenue and rested that morning."

The Hampton Roads Port of Embarkation was also noted for the tremendous quantity of material it shipped overseas during the war. Excellent railroad connections, piers, terminals, and warehouses created by Collis P. Huntington enabled the port to fill 438 ships with 47,000 animals and 4 million tons of supplies.

The Peninsula became one of the largest concentrations of military activity in the U.S. Besides the four primary Hampton Roads Port of Embarkation camps, numerous other installations were created to support the war effort. Camp Eustis, while primarily serving as a coast artillery training base, was also utilized as an embarkation point for over 20,000 men assigned to artillery and motor transport units. Camp Wallace, located in James City County and named in honor of Colonel Elmer J. Wallace, an artillery officer killed in France, was built in October 1918 to support artillery training activities at Camp Eustis. Camp Wallace had 30 barracks, 6 storehouses, and 8 mess halls. A special spur track was built to connect the two camps. Other installations, such as the Yorktown Navy Mine Depot, were hurriedly constructed to support training and to organize the war material required to wage war in Europe.

Even though the Peninsula is best remembered for the men and material shipped overseas through its ports, the region also sent its share of local soldiers to the battle front. Hampton's Battery D was assigned to the 111th Field Artillery Regiment of the 29th Infantry Division following its guard duty in Newport News and was sent to Alabama for training. The battery eventually arrived in France on July 19, 1918, but did not reach the front until November 7, 1918. The Huntington Rifles and the Newport News Light Infantry Blues were merged into one unit and mustered into Federal Service as Company C, 116th Infantry Regiment of the 29th Infantry Division. Many residents were drafted (1,163 from Newport News) while others, such as Ray Clifford of Hampton (pictured here), enlisted in other branches of the service.

Members of the Peninsula's African-American community, including Willie Banks of York County, also sought to serve in the nation's armed forces. World War I was perceived by many African Americans as an opportunity to prove their worth as American citizens through military service. Over 758 African Americans from Newport News were drafted; countless more enlisted. Bigotry and racial injustice relegated over 80% of these men to service in pioneer, labor, or stevedore units. Willie Lee Banks (pictured here), a mechanic in the 811th Pioneer Corps, trained at Camp Lee, Virginia.

Numerous organizations, such as Fort Monroe's YMCA (pictured here), established facilities catering to the social, physical, mental, recreational, and moral well-being of the almost overwhelming influx of soldiers on the Peninsula. The entire community went out of its way to make the soldiers feel at home. During a single month in 1919, the Newport News YMCA provided 2,200 baths, slept 2,475, served 6,000 meals, mailed home $5,675, checked 2,385 parcels, and provided two pool tables where 486 hours of pool were played. A total of 26,255 men used the building during the month.

The War Camp Community Service, the YMCA, and the Knights of Columbus were among a host of organizations that established facilities on or near every camp and installation on the Peninsula. Hostess Houses and Red Circle Clubs provided every imaginable type of entertainment, ranging from teas and plays to concerts and dances. The Knights of Columbus Hall on Langley Field, which opened in December 1918 and was the largest in the entire Air Service, had a motto which typified the actions of service organizations on the Peninsula: "Everybody welcome, everything is free, the door is always open; we've thrown away the key." The Langley Field Knights of Columbus facility, similar to the field's YMCA (pictured here in 1919), offered dancing, movies, plays, music, and boxing exhibitions.

The Red Cross, Salvation Army, Jewish Welfare Board, American Library Association, and the Women's Service League were some of the other associations that attended to the needs of the servicemen in a wide variety of ways. The Women's Service League operated the Hospitality House of Hampton at the Hampton Yacht Club. Organized by Mrs. Frank Darling, the center

provided special lunches and music, "entertaining young ladies," and motherly advice. It is no wonder that one New Zealand soldier wrote a thank you letter to the ladies of the First Presbyterian Church in Newport News exclaiming, "We had the time of our lives in that seaport town."

Dances were by far one of the most popular forms of entertainment. The YMCA reported that it was often "hard to get enough girls" out to the more remote camps like Camp Eustis. The dances were so well attended by servicemen that most of the unattached young ladies on the Peninsula had been "doing the Dance of Death" for over a year. Many considered it their patriotic duty. Even though the dances were all chaperoned by grandmothers and married matrons, there were numerous cases of unchaperoned liaisons that resulted in venereal disease. Public health officials quickly tried to mitigate the problem. A free clinic was opened in downtown Newport News, and a home for "wayward, helpless, and straying girls" was established shortly thereafter.

Due to the influx of so many servicemen on the Peninsula, YMCA work was important to the community. The thousands of soldiers virtually overwhelmed local volunteers; thus, the National War Work Council of the National YMCA had to supplement activities on the Peninsula. The YMCA operated tent facilities at each embarkation camp until more adequate buildings could be erected. Eventually 10 entertainment huts were constructed—one each at camps Morrison, Hill, and Alexander and seven in Camp Stuart (five for whites and two for blacks). A main facility was built on the Casino Grounds. The YMCA invested over $200,000 constructing, maintaining, and equipping these buildings. This is a view of the Fort Monroe YMCA's reading room.

Everyone in the community pitched in to help the servicemen. The owners of movie theaters in downtown Newport News provided free films on Sundays. Permanent installations like Fort Monroe (pictured here) constructed their own theaters. There were other ways to make the doughboys feel comfortable. The Jewish Welfare Board raised $70,000 for war work. These dollars were used to distribute 60,000 letterheads, 30,000 envelopes, and 10,700 packages of cigarettes at Camp Stuart's embarkation hospital. Workers of the Jewish Welfare Board met 76 transports filled with returning troops and distributed 45,970 handkerchiefs, 93,800 "hello" cards, and a countless quantity of matches, chewing gum, and cigarettes.

The Red Cross was perhaps one of the most active humanitarian organizations during the war. The Newport News Chapter was organized on June 2, 1917, with branch chapters established in Denbigh and Morrison. A separate Hampton Chapter was also established in 1917. The Newport News Chapter, however, assumed the herculean task of providing canteen service for the troops moving through the port. The canteen service's primary purpose was distributing coffee, cake, chocolate, cigarettes, and other supplies to the soldiers as they boarded transports, day and night. On June 18, 1918, nearly 8,000 men were fed between 4:00 a.m. and daylight. It was reported that the Newport News Red Cross Canteen fed 40,000 servicemen one month.

The Newport News Chapter began its operations in a vacant Catholic church on Washington Avenue and a former Elks building on Thirty-second Street. A new facility opened for canteen service on River Road and Twenty-fourth Street to be closer to the piers. Mrs. Lelia P. Hudson was the official hostess. Another important facet of the Newport News Chapter was caring for wounded men returning through the port. Not only did the Red Cross workers provide food, newspapers, and other necessities to the wounded, they also traveled with the troop trains to Richmond to help relieve the soldiers from the tedium of the long trip. In preparation for Christmas Day 1918, the Red Cross Canteen prepared almost 50,000 packages to be delivered to transports and naval vessels that were not expected to be in port in time for the holidays.

The Red Cross Motor Corps was an important organization for the entire Hampton Roads area. Established by its captain, Mrs. J.O. Arroll, the corps assumed the duties of transporting all canteen supplies, shipping supplies to transports and hospital trains, and moving the sick and wounded from transports to the Debarkation Hospital at Camp Stuart and then onto hospital trains. Since there was not a canteen service in Norfolk, the Newport News Chapter used the Red Cross Motor Corps to transport workers across Hampton Roads to care for servicemen on the southside. One of the Red Cross Motor Corps volunteers, Elizabeth Elton Weaver, donated her time to the Red Cross and provided the organization with a Dodge truck.

Six

SHIPS FOR VICTORY

The one word that sums up the Peninsula's industrial contribution to the Allied war effort is shipbuilding. Newport News and, to a lesser extent, Hampton both operated shipyards that produced a wide variety of vessels necessary to support the nation's war effort. This is a view of the 1918 launching of the *Kahoka* at Hampton's Newcomb Lifeboat Company.

Homer Ferguson was president of the Newport News Shipbuilding and Dry Dock Co. for only two years before the U.S. entered the war. Ferguson wisely utilized this brief period to prepare the yard for wartime expansion. He anticipated the need for ship repair and stockpiled over $2 million worth of materials and supplies to complete this type of specialty work. Repair work constituted a majority of the shipyard's activities during the war. The repair record was impressive: 144 for the U.S. Shipping Board, 141 for the Army, 118 for the Navy, 160 for the British government, and 437 for private owners. This record totaled 1,000 ships repaired.

"Preparedness" was Ferguson's motto. When Norfolk staged a grand Preparedness Parade on June 17, 1916, Ferguson closed the shipyard at noon so that a large contingent of shipyard workers could participate. Ferguson even established the Newport News Shipyard Band. The band, directed by Walter Keppler, gave noon concerts on Tuesdays and Fridays. Once the U.S. entered the war, it was reported that "Music hath pep to help us whip the Kaiser." An employee newsletter, first titled *Rivets* and then renamed *The Shipbuilder*, was first published in 1918. *The Shipbuilder* provided workers with more patriotic spirit and featured slogans such as "If U work U beat U boats" and "Come, let us warship."

In September 1916, President Woodrow Wilson created the U.S. Shipping Board and its subsidiary, the Emergency Fleet Corporation. This emergency naval construction program had a tremendous impact on the Newport News Shipyard. Over $100 million in contracts were issued to the shipyard between 1916 and 1919. The yard resorted to a round-the-clock production schedule to complete the rush orders for destroyers, battleships, and cargo vessels. Employment figures increased from 7,600 in April 1917 to the peak of 12,512 in September 1919. Extra workers were needed for every kind of task. One of these workers was college student Thomas Wolfe, who worked at Langley Field and in Newport News during the war. He recorded his experiences in his first novel, *Look Homeward Angel*, which included the following reference: "There were strange rumors of a land of Eldorado to the north, amid the war industry of the Virginia coast. Some of the students had been there, the year before: they brought back stories of princely wages. One could earn twelve dollars a day, with no experience. One could assume the duties of a carpenter, with only a hammer, a saw, and a square. No questions were asked."

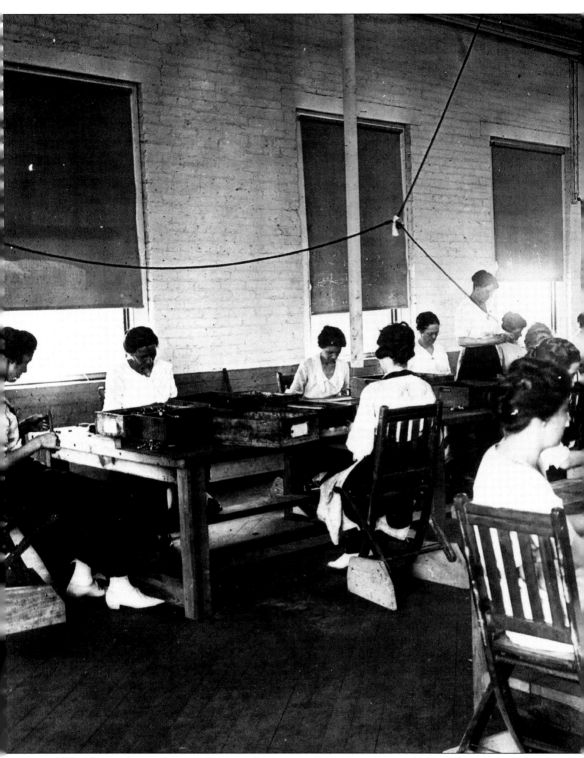

The shipyard's need for workers resulted in employing women to replace the men serving in the armed forces. Most of the women were assigned to tasks associated with ship repair or

merchant vessel construction. When the war was over, these women workers were replaced by the returning servicemen or by contract attrition.

THE SHIPS
ARE COMING

UNITED STATES SHIPPING BOARD ⁘ EMERGENCY FLEET CORPORATION

The U.S. Shipping Board initiated a massive shipbuilding program, resulting in the construction of over 2,300 merchant ships. The Newport News Shipyard constructed 10 of these vessels (totaling 99,610 tons deadweight capacity) during the war, as well as 137 merchant vessels for private owners. As the Emergency Fleet Corporation requested the shipyard primarily to construct combat ships, it produced few merchant vessels. Between April 1917 and November 1918, the Newport News Shipbuilding and Dry Dock Co. completed 1 battleship (the USS *Mississippi*), 4 destroyers, 12 torpedo boat destroyers, and 3 towing targets.

A total of five battleships were ordered for the Navy between 1916 and 1919. Only two—the USS *Maryland* and the USS *West Virginia*—were completed, and this not until the war had ended. The other three battleships were canceled. Once the U.S. entered the war, the Navy ordered the shipyard to defer building battleships and concentrate on destroyers. The hurry-up programs resulted in the shipyard producing 25 destroyers: 5 in 1918, 8 in 1919, and 12 in 1920, as well as 8 tankers. Destroyers such as the USS *Dahlgren* (DD-187), the USS *Goldsborough* (DD-188), the USS *Sommes* (DD-189), and the USS *Abel P. Upshur* (DD-193) served the Navy during the post-war era. Josephus Daniels, secretary of the navy, is shown here at the October 19, 1919 launching of the 1,207-ton destroyer *Bagley* (DD-185). The ladies participating in the christening ceremony are, from left to right, Mrs. Josephus Daniels, Mrs. Adelaide Worth Bagley, Miss Belle Bagley, and Miss Ethel Bagley.

Most shipyard launchings were simple affairs. Even a double launching of a destroyer and freighter in September 1918 received little fanfare. "There was little time for that now," *The Shipbuilder* reported, "and the spirit of the time frowns upon it. Every aim is to get more ships in the water." There was one big event after all in the summer of 1918—the July Fourth Liberty Launching Day. This event was celebrated at shipyards across the country, and in Newport

TO BE LAUNCHED JULY FOURTH
LIBERTY LAUNCHING DAY
THREE DESTROYERS
THREE CHEERS

HULL 226
ABBOT

HULL 224
THOMAS

News it focused on the launching of three destroyers: the *Thomas*, the *Haraden*, and the *Abbot*. Each of the destroyers were called by the *Daily Press* "a death blow to Prussianism." Liberty Launching Day began at 8:00 a.m. when the *Thomas* was launched, and festivities continued with a parade featuring 8 bands, numerous floats, and over 9,000 sailors, soldiers, and civilians. The patriotic event concluded with an evening community song fest on the Casino Grounds.

The shipyard did more than just produce ships for the war effort. As the largest private employer on the Peninsula, the Newport News Shipbuilding and Dry Dock Co. assumed a leadership role coordinating community projects and various types of home front-oriented war work. Homer Ferguson served on the U.S. Shipping Board advisory committee and helped coordinate the design for standardized steel ships. The company contributed greatly to Red Cross activities and other special campaigns; however, the employees themselves gave perhaps the biggest "wholesome swat at the Kaiser" through bond drives. The Fourth Liberty Loan Campaign contributions topped $1 million, which averaged more than $100 per employee. Homer Ferguson summarized this bond campaign by saying that "no other similar body of workers anywhere in the United States have done more towards the winning of the war."

The need for ships during World War I was so great that the Newcomb Lifeboat Co. was established, under the auspices of the U.S. Shipping Boat's Emergency Fleet Corporation, on the south side of Sunset Creek in Hampton. The new shipyard was awarded a contract to build 10 wooden subchasers, each 65 feet in length, for the Navy. A second contract was received to build four wooden-hulled, 350-foot merchant ships without engines.

Although two hulls were canceled, two of the merchant ships ordered, the *Kahoka* and the *Luray*, were launched in 1918. Sunset Creek had to be dredged to accommodate the 18-foot draft of the *Kahoka*, shown here shortly after launching with the *Luray* still under construction. The Newcomb Lifeboat Co. ceased operations once the war ended.

The Peninsula's shipbuilding record during World War I was simply outstanding. Not only were numerous vessels completed in time to support the war effort, none of the ships produced by the Newport News Shipyard were declared unserviceable during the war. Only one Newport News-built ship, the *Tampa*, struck a mine while on escort duty in English waters.

Seven

THE HOME FRONT

The Peninsula's home front activities were equal to, if not greater than, the military actions and industrial work accomplished on behalf of the war effort. People literally opened their doors in every feasible way to the servicemen passing through the port. A special "Take a Soldier Home" program was initiated for Sunday evening dinners. One doughboy recalled that "I never saw such a town and such people . . . that's the fifth invitation today and I can't hold another bit." Bond drives, housing problems, meatless Mondays, and patriotic sing-a-longs were all part of the Peninsula's unique wartime experience. This photograph depicts work crews on Post Street during the construction of Hilton Village.

The women of the Peninsula endeavored to serve as "soldiers without guns" while simultaneously striving to maintain households disrupted by the war. The Women's Service League was organized to coordinate special events and projects. Everyone had a job to do, as Mrs. Russell Syer Barrett commented: "Never before had women been called for such an expenditure of energy and effort . . . Many found it impossible to get domestic service of any kind—and in the meantime the calls of all the many war activities grew. How could one manage! Soldiers home to dinner, paying guests in spare rooms, meetings and all sorts of work outside—and many times no cook. Still we lived to tell it." A patriotic lawn party, one of the many fund-raising events sponsored by the Women's Service League, was held on June 2, 1917, at the Hampton Roads Golf Club. The floral fete's program included a grand parade and the "American Tableau" shown above. Uncle Sam, Betsy Ross, the Three Minutemen, and Mars, the Roman god of war, are surrounded by ladies dressed in costumes from Allied countries, such as the "Russian daisy delegation."

Women joined a variety of organizations, participated in special campaigns to provide comforts for soldiers, and tried to help the ravaged populations in war-torn Europe. Mrs. Henry Lane Schmeltz of Hampton coordinated a drive that raised $3,000 to aid Armenians, and in September 1918, female Red Cross workers packaged 16 boxes of clothing weighing almost 4,000 pounds and sent them to Belgium. Many women volunteered their time as hostesses at facilities such as the River Road Red Cross Hostess House, which was established to aid soldiers.

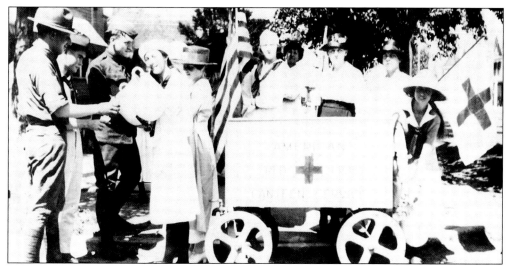

Booths were established by most of the war work organizations, such as the North End Girls' Water Brigade, to provide soldiers with food, drink, and other necessities while they marched to and from transports. An ice-cream fund was initiated when one wounded soldier asked if "there was any way they could get some honest-to-God ice cream." Mrs. E.M. Braxton donated $10 in memory of her son, who started the fund. By September 1919, a total of $6,234 had been collected, and 83,000 soldiers had consumed more than 6,100 gallons of ice cream.

Children also played an important role on the home front. Newport News High School organized a military plan for its students in 1916, and the school was viewed as a "center of the preparedness movement." The cadets, trained by drill instructor Sergeant Bresnahan, marched in most patriotic parades, and 72 students attended a week-long camp of instruction at Grand View in June 1917. D.A. Dutrow, the Newport News superintendent of schools, took an even greater step in support of the war effort when he announced in June 1918 that the "awful German language" would be dropped from the high school curriculum.

The Boy Scouts were one of several children's organizations that contributed to the war effort. In Elizabeth City County, Boy Scouts supported one bond drive by selling 20 Liberty Bonds valued at $1,250. On April 22, 1919, Boy Scouts in Newport News sold $20,000 in bonds during the Victory Loan Campaign.

Young girls also joined in the fight against "Prussianism." A girls' club (pictured here) was organized in Newport News's African-American community offering cooking and sewing classes as well as providing special entertainments for soldiers. The local Jewish community created a "Jewish Girls' Service Club," which had a membership of 55 girls. They presented countless one-act farces for soldiers, served refreshments at the piers, attended dances, and raised $100 for the United War Worker's Campaign. Other organizations, like the Girls' Patriotic League and the Junior Red Cross, knitted socks and rolled bandages during school recess. Junior Red Cross members visited hospitals daily and presented flowers and other gifts to incapacitated soldiers.

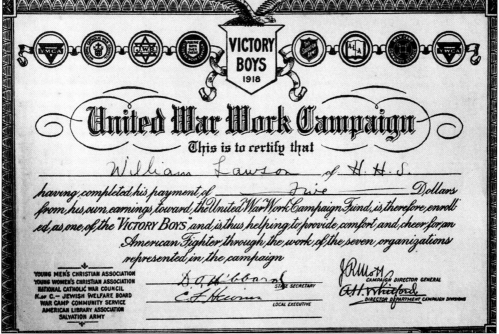

Local schools became a vibrant focal point for patriotic activities. The Domestic Science department of Newport News High School was opened to enable soldiers to get a taste of "mother's cooking," served by the hands of eager students. The English department prepared original stories that were illustrated by members of the Art department. Schools throughout the Peninsula collected magazines and books from the American Library Association for soldiers to read aboard transports. Thousands of peach stones and nut shells were saved to produce carbon for gas masks. Even the butt ends of pencils were donated to soldiers preparing to embark for Europe. Perhaps the greatest contribution was the bond drives. The War Saving Stamps program was a success all across the Peninsula. In one week, students in Newport News purchased, out of their own savings, $13,000 worth of War Saving Stamps.

Virtually everyone on the Peninsula participated in the six major bond drives organized to underwrite the U.S. mobilization for war. The success of the Liberty Loan campaigns in Hampton resulted in $2,100,150 subscriptions, which was almost $20,000 over the quota. This achievement has been generally attributed to women, including Mrs. Bayard Lee, chair of the Woman's Liberty Loan Committee. The ladies of Hampton worked diligently to solicit subscriptions at booths in banks and other public places. Over the course of the war, the citizens of Hampton purchased $96,720 in War Saving Stamps and $11,832.50 in Thrift Stamps. The small community of Phoebus, near Fort Monroe, was not to be outdone. The town's citizenry purchased $17,065 in War Saving Stamps and $2,021 in Thrift Stamps.

The Victory Loan Campaign was the largest fund-raising event. Announced on April 22, 1919, it was the last bond drive. Although the war was over, money was needed for shipbuilding initiatives and to provide humanitarian aid to the war-ravaged Europeans. "Over the Top" was the campaign's battle cry, and a special appeal was made using a "challenge from Flanders Field where heroes sleep for others' sake." Citizens were reminded not to break faith "with those who died." During the drive's first week of subscriptions, patriotic fervor in Newport News reached a fevered pitch, prompted by rallies and special events. Harry Gardiner, "The Human Fly," climbed the courthouse tower, and Army tanks demonstrated on the Casino Grounds how they could have "rolled over the Kaiser." The result was outstanding; the Victory Loan quota for Newport News was $1,677,400 and 11,655 individuals purchased $2,262,450 worth of bonds.

Food production on the Peninsula was primarily of local significance. Even Warwick County's pacifist Mennonites brought their farms into the fight. In Elizabeth City County, the 1918 wheat harvest was the largest on record. The Newport News Chamber of Commerce instituted a home garden campaign. Over 1,000 vacant lots were set aside for amateur gardeners to plant 225 bushels of seed potatoes and 5,000 bags of assorted garden seeds.

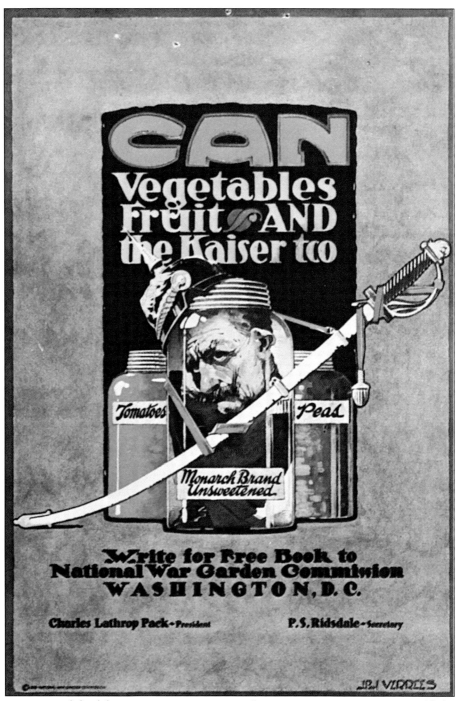

Conservation of food became a major priority. A community cannery was established in Newport News at Thirty-ninth and Washington Streets. The shipyard hired canning expert Annie E. Sale of Georgia to train local women how to conserve their homegrown produce. The project was overwhelmingly successful; over 400 workers prepared 8,932 containers of food in a four-month period.

There was an acute housing shortage in Newport News prior to the U.S. entry into the war, and it became much worse when hostilities intensified the demand for more ships. Between 1910 and 1920, Newport News nearly doubled in population, rising from 26,246 to 47,013. The need for workers at the shipyard only made the situation more problematic. "People who have never before thought of taking any roomers or boards could not resist this opportunity to make money," the 1919 Municipal Survey noted. "Every little shanty became a habitable home and a veritable gold mine for its owner." Boarding houses were filled and workers resorted to "hot-bedding" or "room sharing." Even though the shipyard built temporary barracks and tent colonies (shown above), shipyard officials found it hard to keep older, skilled workers. This circumstance prompted Homer L. Ferguson to testify before the Senate in January 1918 that, because of the housing shortage, the shipyard could not hire enough men to build the ships the government had ordered.

Ferguson convinced the U.S. Shipping Board's Emergency Fleet Corporation to provide financing for several projects in Newport News. One of the first projects was the construction of the Shipyard Apartments (pictured here under construction) on Washington Avenue across from the yard. The complex was designed by noted architect Francis Y. Joannes and incorporated the latest innovations in fire safety, lighting, ventilation, and convenience. The Belfast Vista Apartment complex was also constructed as part of the housing effort on the waterfront between Fifty-third and Fifty-fourth Streets.

More remarkable is the story of Hilton Village, a "planned community" that was truly visionary for its time. Hilton, the first government-subsidized housing project, was designed by renowned town planner Henry Vincent Hubbard of Harvard University. The planned community was built 3 miles north of Newport News city limits in Warwick County on 200 acres of land purchased

by the shipyard. The property, known as the Darling tract, had been occupied by a house called "Hilton" on a bluff overlooking the river. The farm was named by the wife of Lieutenant John Pembroke Jones, CSN, an officer aboard the CSS *Virginia* during the Civil War.

The project began on April 18, 1918, and Hubbard's dream of creating an ideal village of English cottage-style homes soon began to take shape. Francis Joannes served as the architect, and a battalion of laborers went to work building "a complete town—proper houses rightly located and arranged, roads, water, sewerage, fire protection, stores, markets, churches, parks, schools, clubhouses, theaters, playgrounds, play fields, etc." Hilton was formally dedicated on July 7, 1918, and by October 1, over a dozen families were renting houses in the village.

This brick school, located on a beautiful site overlooking the James River, was completed in 1919, and all of the homes were finished by 1920. Each of the roads intersecting Main Street was named after shipyard officials. Following the war, a company was formed to sell the houses. Sales were non-existent; the demand had slackened with post-war layoffs at the shipyard, and many thought the houses were overpriced at $2,800. The first sale did not come until 1922, but eventually Hilton Village became a special community of homeowners.

In addition to the war on the Western Front, the world was stricken with a deadly epidemic in the summer and fall of 1918. Known as the "Spanish flu" because it originated in Spain, this strain of influenza circled the globe, resulting in 12.5 million deaths. Millions more Americans died from the Spanish flu than from battlefield causes during World War I.

It is thought that the Spanish flu was brought to Hampton Roads aboard a steamer that docked at Newport News in mid-August 1918. The entire crew was sick, and due to limited quarantine procedures, the virus quickly spread. The entire Peninsula was filled with transient soldiers moving through the overcrowded camps. The constant flow of people helped to increase the number of infected individuals. By September 1918, the Peninsula was in the midst of an epidemic. Over 5,000 cases were reported in October. It was soon called the "Hun Plague," as many believed it to be an evil German plot to win the war.

The military camps were hit especially hard by the flu. Since there was no known remedy, doctors tried everything to cure their patients. Soldiers at Camp Stuart were "aired" in special breezeway wards, but the cold, damp outdoor accommodations resulted in even more deaths from pneumonia. Members of the Red Cross in Hampton prepared 500 pneumonia jackets for soldiers, and all Red Cross volunteers became hospital workers. Nothing seemed to work. Solomon Travis Jr. recalled that "the soldiers died like flies out there in that mud." A daily ritual of wooden caskets arrived at the C&O depot from Camp Stuart for shipment home.

The situation became so critical that the City of Newport News converted the newly completed Walter Reed High School into an emergency hospital. The Public Health Service donated $5,000, which was matched by the city, to help combat the disease. Movie theaters, hostess houses, and other community facilities were closed as people were urged to avoid crowds. Surgical masks or cotton cloths were worn by many civilians to filter out "flu particles." Nevertheless, funeral homes operated 24 hours a day to process the corpses and still could not keep up with the demand. There seemed to be nowhere to go to escape the flu plague, but by late November 1918 its fury had abated, and the Peninsula returned its focus to the war effort. The Spanish flu was officially declared over in July 1919.

Eight

WELCOME HOME

When the Armistice ending the war was declared on November 11, 1918, a mixed sense of pride and relief was felt across the Peninsula. There was, however, little time to reflect upon peace. The embarkation camps were immediately transformed into reception centers welcoming home the doughboys.

The Armistice Day celebrations on the Peninsula resulted in chaos. The day began as a jubilant occurrence, which was commemorated by an afternoon parade down Washington Avenue in Newport News. Over 1,000 soldiers from Camps Eustis, Stuart, and Morrison participated in the parade, and as they marched through town, they were jeered by some of the on-lookers as "tin soldiers." These jaunts and jeers angered the men, many of whom were already disappointed not to have had the chance to see action on the front. Some were simply disenchanted with several downtown merchants who had engaged in war profiteering and price gouging at the expense of the soldiers. The stage was set for the "Battle of Newport News" when, following the parade, the soldiers all received overnight passes. The men immediately returned to Newport News to enact their revenge.

Thousands of soldiers descended upon downtown Newport News at nightfall and immediately turned Washington Avenue into a war zone. Local police were powerless to stop the riot centering on the various shops that had overcharged soldiers. The enraged doughboys broke windows, looted stores, and created general mayhem. Pawnbrokers' signs were used as bowling balls and barbers' poles were used as battering rams against shop doors that did not open quickly. The Jem Cigar Store suffered the destruction of $1,000 worth of goods, and witnesses watched soldiers dump candy into the street from a confectionary store. The Palace Restaurant was virtually demolished and trolley service suspended. Just one streetcar was permitted to move, only to give a tow to a sailor sitting in a bathtub he had tied to the rear coupling. A giant bonfire was lit in the center of Washington Avenue and fed with anything flammable the soldiers could find. The riot was ended thanks to a wise tactical move by an army major. A rumor was spread about a large fight between civilians and soldiers across the Twenty-eighth Street Bridge. When the marauders arrived on the other side of the bridge, they were met by 300 military police, who closed off the bridge behind them and finally restored order.

The riot was quickly forgotten despite the considerable damage along Washington Avenue. The soldiers were satisfied that they had survived suffering "the siege of Newport News." Civilians cleaned up the streets and then simply redoubled their efforts at hospitality. While one poem was circulated by soldiers declaring Newport News "the rottenest hole the wide world through," another popular song, "Newport News Blues" was written to express more of the homesick feelings the soldiers shared:

> *Oh! Newport News Blues is the lat-est fad*
> *Newport News Blues will surely drive you mad,*
> *You start into jazz,—then you raz-ma-taz-*
> *Oh way down south—in the land of cotton,*
> *Your Uncle Sam has not forgotten,*
> *You're a-way—a-way far a-way from Broadway—*
> *They sing and dance that haunting mel-o-dy-*
> *Oh! When you're down in Newport News,*
> *What do they want to play that dog-gone blues for?*
> *The blues of Newport News . . . —Oh! News.*

The first transport ships with homeward bound soldiers began arriving in mid-December 1918. V. King Pifer, associate Red Cross field director at Camp Stuart, remembered that when the USS *Nansemond* arrived on March 14, 1919, "the cheers of the men on board could be heard for several miles." The scene would be repeated hundreds of times during 1919 as the Hampton Roads Port of Embarkation welcomed home almost a half a million doughboys.

Each ship was greeted by two brass bands playing patriotic melodies. Enterprising photographers captured views of "The Ship That Brought Us Home" for sale to the soldiers as they marched into camp from the transports. A fleet of 34 vessels was organized to return the troops to Hampton Roads. The trip generally took two weeks, but the *Orizaba* and *Sibiney* both made the trip in eight days. Only one shipping mishap occurred; the *Zeelandia* crashed into a pier on May 23, 1919. Fortunately, no one was injured.

A special "House of Extermination" was also constructed at each camp in order to cleanse soldiers from "cooties" upon their return from France. The delousing, more popularly called "de Francing," was a necessary ritual before the soldiers could be sent home. Some of the soldiers even brought back French or Belgian wives, despite official statements that "Yankees Not to Wed French Girls." The women were separated from their new husbands upon arrival in Newport News and quartered at Camp Morrison. The newlyweds were reunited as soon as the soldiers were discharged from service. Numerous local couples were also reunited with the war's end, including Harry and Maggie Forrest Hopkins of Poquoson. They both enlisted and were finally rejoined after passing through the Hampton Roads Port of Embarkation.

Numerous foreign troops, including New Zealanders and Australians, passed through the Hampton Roads Port of Embarkation en route home. There were unusual soldiers, too, such as members of the Czech Legion. These men were former members of the Austro-Hungarian Army, who, once captured, exchanged their POW status and fought in the Russian Army. The Russian Revolution ended the war on the Eastern Front and caused the Czech Legion to move across Russia, often fighting the newly formed Red Army through Siberia to Vladisvostok. The legion's stop in Newport News on July 20, 1919, was just a small part of its long journey home.

A Welcome Home Committee was established by the Newport News Chamber of Commerce shortly after the Armistice. The committee sought to coordinate the activities of civic associations in greeting all transports. Whenever a transport arrived, the city fire and church bells were rung and groups of schoolchildren were sent to wave flags and cheer as the soldiers marched from the piers to the camps. Red Cross Canteen and War Community Service volunteers were always on hand to pass out refreshments and cigarettes. Volunteers were virtually overwhelmed by the returning soldiers. Approximately 384,000 men—21 percent of all the troops returning to the U.S.—were handled through the port of Newport News in this disembarkation role. The Red Cross Canteen fed 422,253 debarking men while also handling 50,000 sick and wounded, who required double duty.

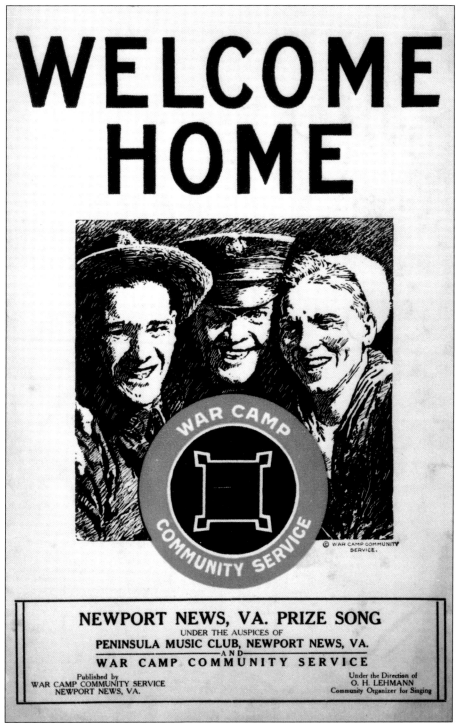

The War Camp Community Service even organized a special contest, in conjunction with the Peninsula Music Club, to publish a "Welcome Home" song. The song was performed countless times at the various clubs and canteens across the Peninsula.

Several states utilized buildings on the Casino Grounds to provide a true welcome home to their units returning through the Hampton Roads Port of Embarkation. Volunteers placed state flags along the road to Camp Stuart. Soldiers could pick up mail and news from home. Telegrams were sent to newspapers back home announcing the safe arrival of their local heroes.

One local resident, J. Hugh Nelson, recalled the parades of veterans marching up Huntington Avenue toward Camp Hill: "Some were bleeding and spectators offered them handkerchiefs. All looked hot, tired and dirty, but in the eyes of the crowd, they were heroes. A merchant with a confectionary store on Forty-seventh Street brought out a tub of ice and crates of sodas. One soldier with a Springfield on his shoulder was wringing wet, and I handed him a cup of water." The soldier gave Nelson a German helmet in appreciation for his thoughtful deed.

On January 6, 1919, the Newport News Chamber of Commerce developed plans to build an "Arch of Triumph" at the intersection of West Avenue. The Newport News City Council supported the concept, and a Central Community Committee was established under the leadership of J. Winston Read. The committee, which included former Newport News Mayor Samuel R. Buxton and Judge John B. Locke, immediately recognized that there was insufficient time and money available to complete the proposed permanent memorial, so it accepted a design by Ralph A. Preas, a shipyard draftsman, based on the Arc de Triomphe in Paris.

Construction of the Victory Arch, as it became known, began on January 27, 1919. The contractor was J.W. Davis. Preas's plans called for a 50-foot-high by 50-foot-wide structure with two 16-foot-square bases and an 18-foot-wide span. The arch appeared massive, but was totally hollow, being fabricated of brick and wood with a plaster facade. Its total cost was $6,081.07, all of which was raised through private donations. An Ohio National Guard unit is credited with being the first to march through the completed memorial. The Victory Arch was formally donated to the city on April 13, 1919, and a portion of Twenty-fifth Street leading to the arch from River Road became known as Victory Avenue.

The Victory Arch was inscribed with the words, "Greetings with love to those who return; a triumph with tears to those who sleep," written by shipyard attorney Robert G. Bickford. The Palm Sunday dedication was a gala affair, complete with over 5,000 schoolchildren waiving small flags. The children, all dressed in white, lined up on the Casino Grounds to spell out the word "Welcome." Aviators Eddie Stinson and Charles Epes flew overhead in a Curtiss Jenny dropping small flags and photographing the event. The keynote speaker, Samuel R. Buxton, summed up the occasion when he said, "The arch is a Victory Arch. It is temporary in character, but what it represents is as eternal as the everlasting hills. Its foundation is laid in the love of a grateful people and the superstructure which has been raised thereon is the outward expression of gratitude of many thousand hearts."

The ceremony culminated with four local Boy Scouts unveiling the arch's inscription. *The Daily Press* editorialized that "The Arch will stand as the guiding light to those who yet are coming here from war, to greet them as they pass on their glorious return."

The largest ceremony planned at the Victory Arch was a commemoration of the return of Virginia National Guardsmen who had served overseas with the 29th Infantry Division. Of particular importance were members of the Huntington Rifles of the 116th Infantry Regiment and Battery D of the 111th Field Artillery. The 29th Division had just been moved up to the front lines when the Armistice was declared. Nevertheless, the entire Peninsula looked to welcome them home as heroes.

The Huntington Rifles were the first to return to the Peninsula. The soldiers debarked from the transport *Matsonia* and became the first Virginian soldiers to march through the Victory Arch. The parade was halted on several occasions when spectators rushed out into the street to embrace their returning loved ones.

Another great patriotic event following the Armistice was the triumphant return of Battery D on May 25, 1919. It was called "the biggest event ever pulled off in Newport News." A flotilla of tugs and other small boats greeted the USS *Virginian* as it neared Newport News Point and then escorted the transport to the C&O piers. The troops debarked under the strains of ship whistles and military bands and marched toward the Victory Arch between columns bedecked with flags and victory laurels. Thousands of schoolchildren once again formed a human "Welcome" on the Casino Grounds as truckloads of young ladies strewed rose petals before the marchers. At a grandstand erected outside the Federal Building, Governor Westmoreland Davis, Secretary of the Treasury Carter Glass, Congressman Otis S. Bland, and Mayor A.A. Moss welcomed the soldiers home.

Battery D turned up Washington Avenue, and the multitude of spectators (the crowd was estimated at over 40,000 individuals) had to be restrained by policemen and Boy Scouts. The day's excitement was reported by the *Times-Herald*: "The cry 'here comes Battery D' arose from everywhere and the great crowd stood on its tiptoes. Then it was that half a hundred fathers, mothers, brothers, sisters, sweethearts, and loved ones broke through the crowds and ran into the ranks to get one of the boys they had recognized. It took only a brief second to find her boy. This happened a number of times as the columns kept coming into view. 'There he is!' one would shout involuntarily and then dart right through the lines, unmindful of guards, unmindful of everything except that she had seen her boy and she was going to him." The article ended by reporting that "Tears were everywhere," and another noted that such a scene "will never be repeated."

On September 19, 1919, two more ceremonies were held at the Victory Arch by the Welcome Home Committee to honor Newport News's servicemen. The first program acknowledged veterans who returned with a commemorative Newport News World War I Victory Medal. A similar, but separate, program was simultaneously held at the Red Circle Club on Marshall Avenue at Twenty-fifth Street to honor African-American veterans. Other Peninsula communities also paid tribute to their hometown heroes with various types of programs. Men like Decauter Carmines of Poquoson, who as a private with the 38th Infantry Regiment was gassed while serving on the Western Front, were accorded all due honor for their faithful service.

The second ceremony at the Victory Arch on September 19, 1919, expressed public gratitude to those soldiers who made "the splendid sacrifice" during the war. Thousands of people attended a solemn tribute that afternoon, which ended with the unveiling of an engraved bronze memorial tablet listing 32 of Newport News's fallen heroes. Once "Taps" was sounded by the bugle, all of the soldiers clasped their hands and pledged to "keep the country safe from all forces of evil for the sake of those who slept in Flanders Field." Eventually, plaques would be added to the Victory Arch honoring fallen soldiers from the entire Peninsula. George Izzard Clopton was one of these men. Clopton was a pre-war James City County resident who served as a private in the Marine Corps in France. He died of his wounds on June 27, 1918.

By the end of August 1919, all of the temporary camps had closed, and the area slowly returned to its pre-war lifestyle. The Peninsula had proven itself time and time again during the war. It was able to provide the ships, manpower, training, sacrifice, and compassion to serve as the leading military community in the U.S. The commitment of the Peninsula's citizens truly helped the nation achieve victory.

Nine

POST-WAR
RETRENCHMENT

World War I brought a major boom to the Peninsula. Extensive shipbuilding contracts, federally funded housing projects, and expanded road systems coupled with new aviation technology and the construction of new permanent military installations all provided the community with outstanding economic opportunities. The Peninsula had become the "harbor of a thousand ships" during the war and was extremely proud of its war service. Many community leaders, as indicated by this 1920 perspective projecting the Peninsula's future growth, predicted that the region would eventually rival New York.

The dream of the Peninsula as an economic powerhouse would not be fulfilled during the decades immediately following World War I. The war simply ended too soon. Local industry fell prey to a post-war recession as the U.S. drifted towards isolationism. Following the war, the Newport News Shipbuilding and Dry Dock Co. secured government contracts totaling $100 million. This seemed to be enough to keep the shipyard working for the next five years, but several ship contracts were canceled in late 1919, and the 1922 Washington Naval Treaty caused the cessation of over $70 million of work. The battleship *Iowa* and cruiser *Constellation*, then under construction, were scrapped in dry dock, and the work force dropped to 2,200. Newport News appeared "like a graveyard"; only Homer Ferguson's underbidding to convert the former German liner *Vaterland* from a troopship into the luxury liner *Leviathan* kept the shipyard open.

The post-war disarmament witnessed several installations greatly reduced, which further weakened the local economy. Fort Eustis was virtually abandoned by the late 1920s, and other bases, like the Yorktown Naval Mine Depot, were maintained on a limited basis (the depot's abandoned airship hanger is shown here). Some area businessmen were able to profit from the closing of the embarkation camps. Newport News businessman and mayor Philip W. Hiden purchased abandoned warehouses near Camps Morrison and Hill and made a fortune shipping tobacco overseas.

Fort Monroe and Langley Field remained the mainstays of the Peninsula's military presence. Fort Monroe flourished as headquarters of both the Coast Artillery School and the 3rd Coast Artillery District. Langley Field trailblazed military aviation technologies during the early 1920s. Langley was headquarters for the 2nd Wing and the Air Service Field Officers School. When Brigadier General William "Billy" Mitchell initiated his controversial campaign to expand military aviation in the early 1920s, he selected Langley Field as a base from which to prove the combat capabilities of aircraft. Mitchell was the outstanding American combat air commander of World War I. He introduced the tactical use of mass bombing against enemy targets. When the war ended, he was appointed assistant chief of the U.S. Air Service and became a strong proponent of an independent air force. The tests headquartered at Langley Field were intended to prove Mitchell's ideas on the use of air power.

Mitchell selected Langley because of its proximity to the mouth of the Chesapeake Bay, enabling him to prove that airplanes could sink battleships. On June 21, 1921, the tests began with Naval Air Service flying boats sinking a captured German submarine. Two days later, bombers from the 1st Provisional Air Brigade sank a destroyer. Tests continued in June and resulted in the sinking of a battleship and heavy damage to a cruiser. In September 1921, B-4 Martin bombers sank three obsolete U.S. battleships. Mitchell proved through his tests that all warships were vulnerable to air attack; however, his efforts to create a separate air force resulted in his court martial. This photograph captured a direct hit of a 300-pound bomb on the *Alabama* during the test on September 24, 1921.

Langley Field also became the post-war center for lighter-than-air testing and training. Balloons and airships, such as the dirigible A-4, were stationed at Langley in the early 1920s.

Several foreign types of airships were stationed at Langley Field for testing. One of these dirigibles was the Italian-built *Roma*. The *Roma* was a semi-rigid airship which gained its buoyancy from highly flammable hydrogen gas. Three attempted test flights were hampered by technical problems. During the fourth attempt, the *Roma* flew over Hampton, Newport News, and Hampton Roads to Norfolk, where the airship plunged to the ground and exploded. The *Roma* disaster ended the Army's interest in large airships.

This photograph, taken at the corner of Main Street and Palen Avenue, depicts army officer George Bland holding his niece Channing in the Coleman family front yard. The image epitomizes the very special bond forged on the Peninsula between the military and civilian communities during World War I. Leaders on the Peninsula learned during the war that the region's economic future was tied to the community's relationship with the military establishment. Even though post-war retrenchment caused severe financial dislocation, the next war would once again reinforce the region's strengths as a springboard and arsenal for global warfare. It was the Peninsula's World War I experience that proved that its citizens, industry, and strategic position were valuable assets to the nation during wartime.

ACKNOWLEDGMENTS

I am indebted to several individuals whose efforts made this important collection of images available for publication. As with previous projects, I must thank my wife, Martha, for typing my text and offering her support. Of course, my son, John Moran, must be commended for his patience. Fellow Virginia War Museum colleagues Sarah Goldberger and J. Michael Moore collected photographs from various public institutions and reviewed the text. In addition, J. Michael Moore organized this collection for publication. Tim Smith, president of the Virginia War Museum's Board of Directors, collected images from private sources and donated his considerable photographic talents to this project. *World War I on the Virginia Peninsula* could not have been produced without their fine assistance.

The following individuals aided the photographic editors and myself: David Johnson of the Casemate Museum loaned us many rare photographs of Fort Monroe and Fort Wool; Michael Cobb of the City of Hampton provided several photographs of Fort Monroe, Hampton, local soldiers, and community military organizations; Joyce Gains of Poquoson aided in the search for photographs of local soldiers; Mike Hatfield, Vice President of Newport News Shipbuilding, generously supplied several photographs of shipyard workers and warships; Kay Phillips of the Yorktown Naval Weapons Station and Tammy Toney of Cheatham Annex provided photographs of the Navy's facilities in York County; and John Pemberton of the Mariners' Museum contributed many images detailing the Peninsula's agrarian heritage, maritime traditions, and wartime mobilization.

PHOTO CREDITS